The Spirit of Joy Church

James McReynolds

Parson's Porch Books
www.parsonsporchbooks.com

The Spirit of Joy Church
ISBN: Softcover 978-1-949888-72-0
Copyright © 2019 by James McReynolds

All rights reserved. No part of this book may be reproduced or transmitted in any form or by any means, electronic or mechanical, including photocopying, recording, or by any information storage and retrieval system, without permission in writing from the publisher.

The Spirit of Joy Church

The Spirit of Joy Church

This book is dedicated to the churches where I served as a minister, 1954-2019.

Woodlawn Baptist Church, Bristol, Tennessee
First Baptist Church, Knoxville, Tennessee
First Baptist Church, Ashland City, Tennessee
Daniel Boone Baptist Chapel, Gate City, Virginia
First Baptist Church, Hallsville, Missouri
Kingsville Christian Church, Kingsville, Missouri
Two Rivers Baptist Church, Nashville, Tennessee
Southminster Presbyterian Church, Nashville, Tennessee
Citadel Park Baptist Chapel, Nashville, Tennessee
Lakewood Baptist Church, Nashville, Tennessee
East Side Baptist Church, Evansville, Indiana
Pilgrim Presbyterian Church, Cameron, Missouri
First Christian Church, Polo, Missouri
Kingston Christian Church, Kingston, Missouri
Zion United Church of Christ, Saint Joseph, Missouri
Camden Point Baptist Church, Camden Point, Missouri
Amazonia United Methodist Church, Amazonia, Missouri
First Presbyterian Church, Savannah, Missouri
First United Methodist Church, Savannah, Missouri
Saint John's United Church of Christ, Amazonia, Missouri
Christ Memorial Baptist Church, Saint Joseph, Missouri
Immanuel Lutheran Church, Saint Joseph, Missouri
Ridgecrest Baptist Church, Council Bluffs, Iowa
Calvary Baptist Church, Glenwood, Iowa
Hillcrest Baptist Church, Omaha, Nebraska
Westminster Baptist Chapel, Omaha, Nebraska
Shenandoah Presbyterian Church, Johnson City, Tennessee
Rich Valley United Methodist Church, Abingdon, Virginia
Washington Chapel United Methodist Church, Abingdon, Virginia
Brick United Methodist Church, Wytheville, Virginia

Contents

Foreword 9
   David H. McReynolds
INTRODUCTION 13
   Grace and Toxicity in Churches
CHAPTER ONE 40
   The Spirit of Fear Church
CHAPTER TWO 50
   The Spirit of Anger Church
CHAPTER THREE 83
   The Spirit of Anxiety Church
CHAPTER FOUR 108
   The Spirit of Guilt Church
CHAPTER FIVE 126
   The Spirit of Joy Church
PRACTICAL APPLICATIONS 139
AFTERWORD 144
   Dr. John Killinger
BIBLIOGRAPHY 145
ABOUT THE AUTHOR 149

Foreword
David H. McReynolds

As a person with a terminal illness, I can understand the spirits of anger, fear, anxiety and joy in ways that can even go beyond the limits of what Jim talks about in his newest book. When you are first diagnosed, you can feel the anger build and the question of "Why me Lord?" ring out loud and clear. Then comes the fear of the unknown. What will this disease do to me and how quickly might it snuff out my life? Living with the illness brings out the anxieties of what will this do to your family and how can you protect them when you are gone. As Jim says, "vulnerability is a deep sacred place . . . it is messy . . . it hurts." In a similar way to Jim finding more than 100 Hebrew words for joy, I fought to find my own joy through these mighty challenges. And I found it through the joy of the Lord, opening my life to Christ Jesus.

When Jim asked me to write the Foreword to his new book, I was honored. I think I know him well since he's my older brother, someone that I have looked up to all my life. He has spent essentially his entire life researching joy and seeking out how to share joy with all those he touches. Through his more than 40 books on joy, he has certainly shared a great amount of knowledge on the subject to the people of the world. No wonder that Norman Vincent Peale ordained Jim "Minister of Joy to the World."

This book matters because of its focus on showing ways that churches stuck in the emotions of anger, fear and/or anxiety might break free of the negative and find and fill their church with the emotion of joy. As Jim states, "the reason God has led me to research and write so many books on joy is to experience how joy can be appropriated in the congregations."

As I read the book, I was reminded of a time when I was either 5 or 6 years old. Jim was talking about Jesus and asked me if I prayed. I told him that "when I prayed, everybody grins." Jim even took this encounter and wrote a brief piece about it in his very first book, Children in my Heart. I think that I was reminded of this instance because of the emotions that I felt as a child. When Jim asked me if I prayed, I was almost afraid to answer – I was fearful of giving the wrong answer. But Jim says that "fear is in fact the intelligent emotion that takes over our bodies and turns us into lifesavers." However, to paraphrase Jim, in the Spirit of Fear congregation, fear has lost its boundaries. I was also anxious. I felt anxiety when I prayed because I saw grown-ups looking at me and smiling. In my young years, I interpreted that somehow as a negative grin. In my case, anxiety caused me to be unable to enjoy the positivity others were showing and being able to truly feel the spirit of God come through my prayers. Jim writes that "anxiety prevents us from realizing that Jesus is already among us." And I think that reality describes this situation well. And I also think I was a little angry at Jim at the time because I thought he was pushing me a little too much about a subject I was not prepared to discuss. But I wouldn't trade those early years with my brothers Jim and Ed for anything the world has to offer. My only regret was that I had too few years with them as they left for college shortly afterward being 9 and 12 years older than I was.

Lastly, I want to encourage you to read the whole of this book at once. It's short enough to do that. Then, I encourage you to take some time to think about its message. Unlike Jim's oil paintings where "the closer look reveals brush strokes, little messes everywhere," a closer look at this book allows the reader to let joy be a surprise, to be a healing emotion, and to be an integral part of a growing and healthy church that is not "crippled in her walk with God because of a lack of the spiritual fruit of joy."

David H. McReynolds

INTRODUCTION

Grace and Toxicity in Churches

If a pastor could dream up and plant the perfect church, what would it be like? Realistically, a minister accepts the church he gets. John Killinger once said, "The trouble with churches are that they fill up with people." All types of people. I dream about a church that is so loving, where my gifts would be valued, and my passions would flourish. My dream congregation would be full of joy. I would never be embarrassed to call it my spiritual home. The church would be so amazing than any non-Christian who visited would never want to leave.

Being an empathic minister and a therapist, I know and understand emotions. Each emotion—fear, anger, anxiety, guilt, and joy according to research—is real and distinct as colors and shades are to an artist.

Emphatic skills are not unusual. Everybody has these skills. We are sensitive and intuitive. We feel what some people never acknowledge. We can't figure out what emotions are. For the past five years, I have traveled to New Haven, Connecticut to share in a twelve-million-dollar study of joy funded by the Templeton Foundation.

Through more than 60 years as an ordained minister and licensed mental health practitioner, I and my clients have experienced healing inside all human emotions. We can only move forward and understand at deeper levels, connecting to ourselves, other people, our life vision, and our purpose.

Most of us learn to shut down emotion as we learn to talk. By age four we squelch emotions in social situations. We are inauthentic with one another. So we lie about our feelings, leave out important words, and trample over the emotional cues of others. Every culture holds unspoken rules about emotions. We do this to survive our social worlds. We tend to label emotions as good or bad. Early in life, we view emotions as acceptable or unacceptable, right or wrong, but few learn an approach to emotions that explain them in enlightened ways.

In my own life, I found that healthy anger is a boundary for our souls, but information about anger focuses on unhealthy states of fury and rage, or anger turned inward as apathy, depression, or resentment. Fear can be healthy as we face dangers. This too goes against most accepted beliefs about fear. Even joy can be dangerous if joy is seen as a choice, as the only emotion we can hold.

Emotions need to be unfrozen, not vilified or glorified. Both perspectives are inappropriate. Nobody should banish some emotions to an underworld. Seek a healthy middle ground where you can express God-given feelings. If we repress emotion, we cause it to go inward. We do not know what to do. All emotion is inside us. In my service as a mental health practitioner in places like drug and alcohol centers, youth and family services, and as a psychiatric therapist, I observed that this repression results into things such as tics, compulsions, psychological or psychiatric illness, neuroses, and addictions. Repressing emotion leads to utter unhappiness and inner pain.

Healthy people let their emotions flow, move, and resolve themselves. Receive all your emotions as you attend to issues at hand, resolve them, and go your way with no regrets. Remember all emotions including joy will pass through you naturally if we let them flow.

An intention to be loving is not enough. Happiness in life comes from learning new ways to deal with our emotions. Repression is emotional numbness. We numb ourselves to feelings so we can think we are comfortable. This numbness spills over into the rest of our lives. We lose our passion, our aliveness, our enthusiasm. Life becomes predictable and boring. Sure, pain may be gone, but life isn't joyous either. Ministers fear a church with unusually difficult circumstances. Some are desperate to be called or appointed to any church. They become so enmeshed that the dysfunctions are accepted as normal. The pastor questions her fitness for ministry. It is impossible to escape shouldering the blame or questioning the call or doing what is appropriate or effective. She suffers nightmares and physical issues in her body.

What concerns me is the many ministers I meet who are emotionally numb. Most are not aware that they have lived in such a way that they do not understand emotions. When we ask them how they feel, they might say, "I feel," but the say words that are statements of facts or what they think. They can be called successful, especially in their culture or setting, but their emotions are in a deep freeze.

As we encounter and observe these leaders, their body language, facial expressions, and tone of voice give signs of emotions, but they are not aware enough to identify them. Their inner world is not in sync with their exterior behavior.

I have written and published more than forty books on the emotion joy. I call my dream congregation, Spirit of Joy Church. How would we describe church? I have found that the churches and their leaders would take emotions seriously. They need a clear identity and vision. In churches of all sizes and denominations that I have served, I find that an effective vision is to create an atmosphere where joy and miracles happen.

The strength of the Christian faith depends on healthy, spiritually nourishing congregations. Congregations are the cradle of the juices of joy where children of all ages are supported and prepared for lives of service that will flourish with the highest happiness.

Significant research is now being done on emotions and their role in making decisions, plus their place in healing, maintaining, and deepening relationships. When I attempt to imagine the church that I want to be a part of, the community that with the joy of Jesus as my strength, I desire to help create, I visualize a church that is honest, loving, capable, wise, and able to accept and deal with the full range of emotion and life experiences. It faces its own fears and is unafraid. The group can be angry in the face of rejection, injustice, and oppression. The church would face the reality of living in a world hungering for love.

Congregations are in a constant place for change. Flourishing congregations successfully deal with the emotions and reality of change. Members come and go, pastoral leadership, lay leadership, needs of the community shifts. The fast pace of change in our culture makes for more response to change.

We are influenced by memories and experiences we do not remember or understand. These emotional tangles of emotions, thoughts, or behaviors. These "non-experienced experiences" encode the unhappy, negative events from our pasts. These repeated patterns keep repeated in each generation. Those tangles become ingrained in our lives and in our churches showing up in upsets, reactions, and problems. If we can identify these patterns, we can understand just how they become the basis for unhappy, negative actions in ourselves and in the church community.

Phil Moffitt analyzed what is possible, He said, "To call the moment when we fully realize that a change is achievable, we realize the imaginative possible. When we are able to envision that an alternative is real, we experience a sudden energetic surge toward actualizing it, which becomes self-reinforcing."

Events hidden but real in the past influence the ongoing response and interpretation bring new awareness in the present. Healing of souls begins with our thoughts. If we fail to see important aspects of the current situation, we will continue to be blind to possibilities.

The Christmas Carol by Charles Dickens tells a story about waking up in life. It can be read as a spiritual guide to help us see what spiritual awakening may look like. In the book, the old miser Ebenezer Scrooge experiences vivid visitations from the ghost of Jacob Marley, his business partner from the past. Scrooge also experiences ghosts from the past, present, and the future. Dickens gives the reader examples of how delusion, past patterns, and hated can be spiritually transformed by insight and compassion. Scrooge was enabled to achieve what we need transforming the structures of personality that traps us in our own misery.

A church in a toxic environment has a high staff turnover, unusual secret keeping, or a major membership rift or exodus.

 Some change beyond normal limits of their imperfection and begin to showcase dysfunction that brings harm not healing. Members squabble over power. Abusers are protected while the victims are ignored. We cannot assume that most churches are healthy. Churches change into authoritarian and dictatorial places. They change into religious addicts at war with the world to protect their own territory.

They stealthily commandeer the leadership positions of the church. In searching for a church where we can be true to the faith, and not get imprisoned in an atmosphere where negativity and abuse continue to persist.

There is no magic bullet for restoring a church back to health. There is no guarantee that things in the church will not get uglier before they get better. They will keep complaining and fighting to get their way. A few can keep from any other member gain access to leadership and they protect against others challenging or participating in it. The doors are guarded by gatekeepers who attempt to identify people seeking to join in by labels or categories, and on that basis decide who is in and who is out.

In this resource, I attempt to describe churches and the type of emotion that prevails. I call them by the names of Spirit of Fear Church, Spirit of Anger and Spirit of Anxiety Church, Spirit of Guilt Church, and the Spirit of Joy Church.

Understanding emotions is to experience what is within persons but what is between them. Emotional affect provides a way to interact with one another. Fear, anger, anxiety, guilt, and joy reflect dispositions toward and human response. If humans lived in complete isolation, we might not need to express emotions. A church shares the tragedy and trauma of living as well as joys and celebration. The congregation's theology and teaching involve how to express the emotions in human relationships. In most churches, the people have never learned about joy. Their lives may have not been experienced as deeply sad, tragic, or abusive. They just have never learned how to be joyful. These interventions are more than the ability to feel serene in the present moment. We must be willing to open up and accept our emotional experiences. A key expression of this is the discovery of emotional intelligence which enables us to understand and to manage our human feelings. This is difficult re-parenting of adults. It is like pulling logs out of us or simply splinters. We probe the inflammation to discover what is sharp and painful. Deeper knowledge comes from our images and body sensations and narratives. Our emotions what we are so foolishly holding on to and where we need to grow into maturity.

When I went for study at the Russian Theological Academy in Saint Petersburg with a cousin, James C. McReynolds who has traveled to Russia many times, I studied Rembrandt's painting and his portrayal of lostness. The older brother is the climax of the parable to whom Jesus speaks about. In the painting, the older brother is dressed richly as his father. In his gold embroidered clothing, he looks angry, judging, annoyed at the father's joyful reception of the youngest son who disgraced the family.

When we deny or repress anger, we become like the older brother. He shows rage. Now we can understand the emotion anger. Certainly rage is understandable. The older brother has stuffed his anger for years, but now he explodes. He wants to get back or to get even. When any of us go inward with anger, our souls will swallow thousands of hours of unhealthy anger.

Until it turns to depression, self-mutilation, substance abuse, promiscuity, insomnia, headaches, or ulcers. Many become passive-aggressive. We are neither hot nor cold, just existing. Outwardly directed anger produces anti-social behaviors, aggression or just being a difficult person.

The emotion anger is quite complex. Most of the time people do not even realize why they are angry or upset. What is this angry experience really about? Where is it originated? Does it come because of something in my past?

The lost older brother grumbles to his father, "This son of yours." Never admitting he is my brother. He is a judger, fault finder, condescending, proud, and self-righteous. A healthy older brother has had opportunities to process his anger. However, in the parable, he remains angry and resentful.

When the older brother hears the music, he says immediately, "Why wasn't I informed? What is this about?" He has a fear of now being excluded. He cannot find any joy, lightheartedness or spontaneity. Those in the Spirit of Anger Churchdom not let go of offenses. They envy others. They act crabby.

Christian tradition pronounces anger as one of the deadly sins. The other six: gluttony, lust, avarice or covetousness, pride, and envy. Those seven deadly sins are temptations for every human. This list gives a useful way for understanding anger. Features of those seven deadly sins are also common in the emotion anger. Every one of the other six can lead us into anger. In the struggle with anger, we do well to study anything in its vicinity.

In Proverbs, we read, "Pride goeth before a fall." Proud people are angry at anyone who challenges their revision of proper human proportions. How dare you not to view me as the greatest? The petulance of tyrants with their people, celebrities with their fans, and clergy with their congregations, is a direct result of pride, as it gives vent to anger. Hold a mirror up to a midget who imagines herself as a giant, and she will smash the mirror or put out her eyes.

Anger is close to the deadly sin of envy. That anger arrives when one imagines others faring better than she is. The enigma of anger is to perceive the world as fundamentally unjust and particularly unjust to her.

Traditionally, in the past, writers always wrote the words, "he, him, man," and in our day in the church, men and women are angry. In one of my Visionquests, the men said they had no idea what their place was in the church. They are angry at women. Some women are envious and angry at the way they have been treated unjustly. All the deadly sins have an element of inability and a stubborn refusal to be satisfied.

Lust and gluttony are often expressed with sensuality. With these sins, angry people hate the way others find delight. Lust is seen as a basic human need. If sensuality brings no pleasure, offense is taken to the body, to a partner, and speaking of lust is worded in violent terms. Sexuality is seen as a sport or an activity of raging fury. Gluttony brings wrath as one observes an eater who is visibly irritated when food fails to arrive at the table as quickly and hot as is desired. Waiters and waitresses view this anger each day.

There is an epidemic of denial about lust. This is mostly a sin of silence. The response in our day is, "You are overreacting." The church has made it clear that nobody believes victims. Sadly, churches fail to protect victims of sexual abuse. The church culture may believe strongly in the sanctity of sex. Diagnosing the scope of this sin isn't easy. Christians have a choice. They can face this deadly sin, and care for the victims.

Or they can just ignore it. Generations of silenced victims will learn that the church is not a safe place.

Sloth and avarice in our day is the couch potato as opposed to the go getter. American families look dead in front of their televisions. Avaricious people work to obtain a prosperous state beyond normal needs, beyond hope, married to a job. In families the slothful spouse and the avaricious spouse are absentees. They enjoy nothing. Those who attempt to love them find bereavement. They are just as good as dead.

Anger and fear are close companions. Sometimes we are angry because we are afraid. Fear paralyzes and anger prepares for action. Acting out of anger often is more dangerous than not acting because of fear. An effective way to deal with anger is to deal with it indirectly by overcoming a fear.

Priscilla Keene of Bristol, Tennessee sent me this anonymous essay on the church. I have used it to introduce some of my weekend Visionquests for Joy. "Church is hard. Church is hard for the person walking through the doors, afraid of judgment. Church is hard for the pastor's family who are under the microscope of an entire body. Church is hard for the prodigal soul returning home, broken and battered by the world. Church is hard for the girl who looks like she has it all together but does not. Church is hard for the couple who fought for the entire ride to the service. Church is hard for the single mom, surrounded by couples holding hands. Church is hard for the widow and widower with no invitation to lunch after church. Church is hard for the deacon with an estranged child. Church is hard for the person singing worship songs, overwhelmed by the weight by the lyrics. Church is hard for the woman insecure as a young leader. Church is hard for the wife who longs to be led by a righteous man. Church is hard for the nursery volunteer who longs for a baby to love. Church is hard for the single woman and single man praying for a mate. Church is hard for the teenage girl wearing a scarlet letter, ashamed and broken. Church is hard for the sinners. Church is hard for me. Church is hard because on the outside it looks shiny and bright. Church is not a building, mentality, or expectation. Church is a group of sinners, saved by grace, living in fellowship as saints. Church is a body of believers bound as sisters and brothers by eternal love. Church is holy ground where sinners stand as equals before the throne of God. Church is a refuge for broken hearts and a training ground for warriors. Church is a converging of confrontation and invitation as hearts seek restoration. Church is a lesson in faith and trust. Church is a bearer of burdens and a giver of hope. Church is a family coming together, setting aside differences, forgetting past mistakes, rejoicing in the smallest of victories. Church is a body, a circle of sinners turned into saints.

Church is a place where hard days are shared such as being at odds with a friend, bearing burdens heavier than my heart can handle, masking the pain with a smile, walking in afraid and broken, I'll remember that God has never failed to meet me in my church."

The New Testament is not just about the teachings of Jesus. The saga of the work of the church which Jesus initiated. If we get rid of the church, we are getting rid of Jesus. Even the idea of church brings despair. Jesus started the church with imperfect people. Broken people brought the grace of God to humans in need of redemption. God is bigger than our wrong choices and all the injustices of the word. Jesus told us we would have trouble in this world. Jesus also noted we can rejoice as He has overcome the world. When we choose to get upset and bothered because the churches are never perfect, we are at least a big part of the problem.

When Christians become members of a church, the expect to discover a congregation will become a second home, a supportive faith group. They can become acquainted and comfortable. They notice how the members do church. Sometimes it takes just a Sunday visit or two before they find a welcoming fellowship, community service, and love leading to growth. Quickly they can put a finger on why the congregation does not lead up to expectations. They find traditions that are unchangeable. Worship does not lead people close to God. Some are just plain toxic. A toxic church is spiritual poison.

It is time for the churches to study and create an atmosphere that makes for Christ-like members who are fallible humans. These churches of every and no denomination take on atmospheres and environments that leads to so much of the unhappiness and pain.

Our expectations that other people can attain what is really beyond humanity cause us to be deeply disappointed and alienated. There is realistic potential for more pain and disappointment. Becoming a member of a church, we can discover a depth of joy that can only be found that can only be found in life together. Churches compete with each other focusing on perpetrating itself rather than on Jesus. They say that they are the only ones who are right.

These churches may be desperate to retain the old members and they struggle to attract new people. The congregation becomes a place where one could lose their faith. Emotions are temporary feelings that dominate our state of mind. Emotions are whimsical, tyrannical, and capricious. It is saddening to me that disposition and attitudes are controlled by them. Negative feelings upset the joy we have expected. They often contradict our faith, mock our witness, and cause havoc. We fall into disillusionment by hurtful environments where the problems are severe. Those negative emotional walls close in around us and emotions get out of control. In a class on Black Preaching at Vanderbilt, we studied the works of James Cone. His outlook defined the way joy and despair were intertwined in the black religious experience. Cone said that trouble was an affirmation of faith that teaches that God is the companion of those who suffer. Trouble is not the last word on human existence.

During one of his Schools of Practical Christianity, Dr. Norman Vincent Peale told of a conversation with Cy Young. Young had retired, but still keep interest in the game. Peale asked, "What do you think about modern pitchers?" He said, "Some of them are really good. Some prance around in their pride. I think they are sissies. When they get into trouble, they are taken out of the game and relieved. Some don't pitch again for several days. I pitched several days in a row. If I got into trouble, they keep me pitching. They told us now pitch your way out of trouble." Pitching out way out of trouble speaks to pitchers of faith.

Some toxic churches are full of cliques. There are small groups of friends exclude others or refuse to give others a chance to join their circle. I once did some coaching with a church that thought another church was exclusive of giving youth anything but trouble. They formed their own youth group made up of the best athletes, popular cheerleaders, gifted students, and most were from wealthy homes.

Some churches make it clear that the only people invited to join them for Sunday brunch are those who are in their personal circle. This atmosphere does not create Christian love nor do new people continue and they go find another welcoming church.

The demographics of today's churches are often characterized by having only under 40 people in a place where retirees are focused inward. Many cater to over 50s and decide to keep themselves as they were 75 years ago. They sing the same songs and the 1950's bulletins could be used this Sunday morning. The hymns and order of worship have never changed. have not changed one iota.

Churches without children will not survive. With no families with their kids a church is reflecting warning signs that something is toxic. The pastor might only preach fire and brimstone which results in the children experiences nightmares. Churches are architects of culture. Shaping a healthy culture is to be aware of toxic culture and healthy culture. In the toxic congregation, we must play politics. Decisions are rarely made in an acceptable way. The real decisions are made in the parking lot.

A golden rule for conflict is to always talk to the person involved directly. Toxic churches spread unhealthy gossip. That is like pouring gasoline to put out a fire.

Conflict is a normal part of any church. Church fights should not exist. Toxic congregations are in perpetual fighting modes. The fights might involve something as trivial as the color for the new carpet. The most powerful members gang up on the pastor or other members. Sometimes the deacons or elders or a board will ask to meet with the pastor somewhere other than the church.

Today's culture is statistical. As entertainment, political fake news, relationships, superficial or bias facts clog our minds, society looks for a way to signify success. Toxicity does not report or describe quality, but only quantity. Churches get too competitive. Success is inherently linked with the competition for numbers. Quality suffers when the main focus is on quantity.

All churches in all places is harmed when local churches compete with one another to have the most members. This competition causes to gain members by sheep stealing from other congregations. People are held hostage to the desires and self-interests of consumers. Giving the world what they desire may satisfy some, but this makes it difficult to give them what they truly need. Seekers hop from church to church over time. Committed Christians keep looking for more, as they search for truth, reality, authenticity and the Good News. They want joy worthy of their destiny.

Against the toxicities of our milieu, the Kingdom of God creates an alternative society. A believer needs to be in a caring community of faithful people who offer guidance, the perspectives of the Bible, wisdom, and love to nurture character growth. The Spirit of Joy Church teaches children the meaning of a community gathering for worship. Teach them why we do specific acts in worship to enable them to enjoy the depth of symbols, the awe of spiritual ritual, the value of silence, the importance of scripture to teach us how to live in the kingdom.

Some congregations ordain people who announce that they heard to call to preach and they become pastors. Charles Spurgeon was ordained at age 17. He died in his 50s. Churches today ordain overeducated yet underequipped professionals. In some denominations, ordination means jumping through many hoops. One would have to about 40 years old before being fully ordained.

At one time in modern church history, church attempted to have at last one of these professionals in every congregation. Many could not serve communion or preach unless they were fully ordained or with a special depensation from a board or higher up in order to accept those responsibilities. Often the body of Christ atrophies. Leaders in most New Testament congregations had special gifts.

A young person who grew up in a middle size or large suburban church may spend thousands to go through seminary training, and she is placed in a rural or tiny congregation. She feels like a fish out of water. In so many places, this arrangement is just not working. Most seminaries are highly academic teaching Hebrew and Greek, church history, Christian Ethics, denominational history and polity, archeology, pastoral counseling, church administration, and for years one received the Bachelor of Divinity degree after eight to years of formal studies. One of my friends threw his Hebrew Bible into the ASB Bridge in Kansas City declaring he would never use it again. Few seminaries equip people to become pastors.

Dr. Tex Sample, who taught at many seminaries including Saint Paul, a United Methodist seminary in Kansas City, once evaluated seminary graduates as "unfit to pastor real people." In my own career as a Methodist elder, I was given the responsibility to serve a six churches circuit charge in the Blue Ridge Mountains in Virginia. The congregations were radically different from each other. One small church was named the Brick Church. When I arrived to start ministry, a lay leader said to me, "We told them we didn't want no educated preacher, and then they sent us you." The primary strength of seminaries is one that is not required for raising up effective pastoral ministers.

Most congregations today are quite small. The average church among the many thousands in the United States has about 40 members. Whether a congregation has a weekly attendance of two or 2,222, they need leadership that is culturally aware, practical, and most important, affordable.

Congregations are relational. Most use the word family, but some single or untraditional families are not given love or acceptance. What I have been naming the Spirit of Joy Church can be any size as they love and accept God's children.

A congregation that is safe and caring of its "children" small or large does not just happen. We must open the door for discussion within the church and in the community. People need permission to discuss difficult subjects. Until churches realize that it is not only permitted but expected that hard subjects are part of ministries, they will avoid any discussion. Both boys and girls fall victims to sexual abuse in churches. When a boy is seduced and abused by a woman, he may not recognize it as abuse. Boys experience crushes on attractive female teachers. Sometimes that relationship becomes sexualized. Ignorance and silence on sex still prevails in many churches.

In thousands of current books, authors emphasize male abusers. Most studies do not mention women abusers. It is more difficult to detect. Women are described as the nurturers of children. It is a misconception that only a few women abuse children. Sexual, psychological, and spiritual abuse are committed by women the same as those perpetrated by men. Women who target children and youth are products of difficult childhoods. Abuse has become normalized in their minds. As adults they get into abusive and unsatisfying intimate relationships. Often the targets are the youth acting as a peer. She has many teen-age friends who she prepares by cajoling and manipulating seeing them as the answers to her many personal needs. Clinical therapists report that these women have much greater pathology than male abusers. A church of any size or denomination must face these issues. If a minister has 100 in attendance, she is addressing 15 or 20 people with dysfunctional abuses within the families of the congregation.

The Spirit of Joy Church

Having only two or three persons attend worship is a much greater challenge than with even 60 or 70. In my own years of ministry, I preached to only one other person 17 times. Back in the 1970's I served Pilgrim Presbyterian Church in Cameron, Missouri. I also served as a therapist at the Saint Joseph State Hospital. One Sunday afternoon, I was asked to preach and lead worship for Warich Chapel. Only one woman came for worship and she seemed "out of it." I gave her my sermon and sang some spiritual hymns. She smiled and left the chapel. On the day of her dismissal from the state hospital, they asked her what things were helpful to her. To my surprise she said, "The Warich Chapel services brought me a lot of joy."

People will drive great distances to attend a particular church. When I served as pastor in Weeping Water, Nebraska, families drove from Lincoln, Omaha, and even Kansas City. Some have family ties or a sense of calling to that congregation that brings them "a lot of joy."

By grace, any congregation can give "the joy of the Lord." Where else could your five-year-old daughter play a piano piece for worship? Where else could a 99-year old woman still lead a choir or play hymns on an old out of tune piano? The Spirit of Joy church is one where the people hang together with patience, joy, and love, learning to live together with old common difficulties. The relationships and the intimacy may have taken years to develop. Size or wealth are not the only things that matter

Many congregations tend to experience high clergy turnover. These are places of limited size, negative self-images, financial constraints, so pastors move on to greener pastures, which means a larger, more affluent congregation. Clergy have conflicting emotions when involved in supporting families with deep problems.

Success is measured numerically. This erodes the self-esteem of pastors and causes congregation to feel inferior as they report numbers in single or small digits.

Denominations, family, colleagues, or self can leave pastors feeling little worth and personal effectiveness. There is a deep gap between her vision and reality with which she must live.

In nearly seven decades of ministry, I have made many mistakes. I have encountered many difficult people including anxious parents in in children and youth work, frustrated volunteers, those with entitlement or power issues. Every congregation has people bringing real problems that are real challenges. Conflict is inevitable. Knowing this truth removes the surprise factor and leaders can be less rattled with confusing emotions. Keeping our cool in difficult situations will make or break our testimony. How many of my counseling clients have been burned as they fuel the fire? Even a single wrong word or reaction can escalate quickly. We must try to protect ourselves. In many difficult atmospheres, I have taped Proverbs 15:1 to my phone, "A gentle answer turns away wrath, but hard words stir up anger." Brushing off a potential viable criticism can diffuse the inflaming situation. Owning our part and offering a gentle word is necessary in hard situations. Clergy are dedicated with change and healing. There is a tear in the soul of clergy if they are not able to make a significant difference in the lives of their parishioners. Patterns of living are generational, and intervention to change those patterns is complex and lengthy. It is not easy to keep in mind that all that has been done is that the church and pastor have been concerned enough to get them help. Being non-anxious can help to not getting pulled into their emotional and spiritual crisis by feeling that the clergy is also experiencing a crisis. I coach clergy to "stay out of the fool's ring."

Hurt people hurt people. Churches can be filled with broken people. Being kind in spite of the bad attitudes of others softens many bad situations. If we become over filled with negative emotions, we can just walk away to gain space and perspective. We and those stirring conflict need to cool down and gather our thoughts and feel our emotions. Walking away can result in coming back collected and prepared for the next step.

As I attempt to give some insight into church dynamics, I am not implying that there is a perfect church. If you are still searching for the perfect is a restless journey. The Westminster Confession of Faith has this statement, "The purest churches under heaven are subject both to mixture and error."

In the Acts of the Apostles 6:1, we read, "And in those days, when the number of disciples multiplied, there arose a. murmuring of the Grecians against the Hebrews."

God through humans calls or appoints us to imperfect congregations to use your gifts, graces, and talents to help the church get a little closer to what God wants. Like some of my oil paintings, they look good from a distance. The closer look reveals brush strokes, little messes everywhere. Until we get to heaven, every single congregation will have brush strokes. Scripture calls these "spots and wrinkles."

CHAPTER ONE

The Spirit of Fear Church

Fear is a signal. It brings a message of a perceived or real danger. Fear does invite people to examine whether the danger is real or imagined. The Fearful Church majors on being anxious, confused, stressed out, discouraged, insecure, submissive. The church appears as isolated. In churches such as this one, they rarely engage in ecumenical activities such as those concerning thanksgiving, Easter, or Advent, or association with other churches. Fear is used as a tool for a dominate group to keep others in subordinate places.

Healthy people buy insurance. They do not speed. They buckle seat belts and pay taxes. Most churches lock their doors at night. Their hours are from 11-12 a.m. on Sunday morning.

All churches have felt true fear. We cannot survive without it. The Spirit of Fear Church has lost its ability to identify fear. Fear is in fact the intelligent emotion that takes over our bodies and turns us into lifesavers. Fear then is freely flowing. The people need to be taught to identify fear when it flows. When danger appears, fear is a constant companion in all situations. So what has happened to fear? In healthy groups, we see that we have survived. The fear retreats and calms so we settle ourselves down. Feelings of fear and anger are closely related. Anger leads to trouble with fear. In the Spirit of Fear Church, fear is activated when there is change. They accuse you or authorities of plotting against you. So they stifle themselves and never speak about their troubles. They may experience panic attack cycles.

The Spirit of Fear congregations need to allow fear to take its secure position inside some well-defined boundaries. The result can be focus, calm, readiness, and energy. They will not appear "fearful" at all. They can heal and allow a healing flow. Fear can then be the energy and focus needed to deal with change or novel situations.

Most Christians cannot have the perspective or understanding of fear as a blessing. In Mark 4:40, the question is sked, "Why did you fear? Where is your faith?" The Spirit of fear Church lets fear sit in the driver's seat.

Pastors of fear put job security above everything. Fear dreads the wrath of lay or denominational leadership. They make life miserable for everybody. The Spirit of Fear Church does not rock the cultural boat. They never attempt anything that has not been done before. They fear doing anything that might be questioned. The status quo is the proper path. The Spirit of Fear rejects change. They give in to any threats inside or outside the local congregation. Fear dominated congregations will not take a chance on troubled or sinful people. Fear never steps out of the cultural boat. Their fears are unreasonable.

As a psychotherapist and clergy coach, I have held the hands and saw tears of pastors who have been deeply hurt and abused. Some families never recover. Divorces happen. Mental illness is chronic. Churches use to talk a lot about clergy killers. With so much competition for pastor jobs, some will go serve any church, and fearful congregations know this. Suicide, breakdowns, and premature aging are realities. The oppression and devastation occur in progressive or liberal, fundamentalist or conservative churches. I shall discuss the Spirits of Anger, Anxiety, Guilt, and then the Spirit of Joy Church.

Some are justifiably afraid of accepting another church. Some never attend a church again. Family members often suffer from ecclesiophobia or an irrational fear of churches. Once when I was pastor of a church in Nebraska, our church reached out to a camping park near the church. Most of the time as we asked them to attend our Sunday worship, they would answer, "Yes, we'll be there." Few came. One of the campers was a former pastor and his family. To appease me, he said they would come. The children looked anxious. Before

I left them, one daughter said, "Oh Daddy, you said we would never have to go inside a church again."

Churches are silent on many issues. Clergy killers is one that is just accepted and is rarely addressed. There are so many reasons as to why some may be fearful toward certain churches. Within Christianity as well as other world religions, there has been the thought that religion is the prime cause of human evil and suffering. Those who fear churches are not all atheists. Much of the division and cruelty, the quarrels and insanity found today are the result of one denomination of Christians or other religions and religious sects being fear-based or disapproving of another group.

In my therapy work, I know that ecclesiophobia is reflected as some find it difficult to pass by a church building on the street or even just to look at a picture of a church, or even to think about one. These children of God experience anxiety, anger, fear, and deep anger and depression as a result of their experience. Similar to those with agoraphobia, they alter their path around town to ensure that they are not in the sight of any church. They choose to live where there are no churches.

Some are extremely fearful of organized religion. In severe cases, they become actively trying to abolish all organized religion. Most experience avoidance.

Avoiding what is feared is a common symptom in any sort of phobia. I have discovered most phobic clients are often out of touch with reality. Those suffering have all experienced a traumatizing event. Few therapists understand ecclesiophobia. Exposure therapy, talk therapy, and even medication can reduce the symptoms. Also talk therapy can be a method for discussing productive ways to cope with panic attacks from the church-based trauma. This would include discussing the underlying reasons to find why they have now become fearful of churches. Uncovering these thoughts makes it easier to treat the specific symptoms associated with this phobia. Talk to a doctor or psychiatrist before you invest in treatment or take any medication.

Most of those who experience the Spirit of Fear Church find tightness in the chest, trembling or shaking, stomach and digestive issues, increase in heart rate, high blood pressure, dryness in the mouth, pale skin. These are signs that you are not sure what you are feeling. Some fear in churches can be positive. A church that is spending all its income or endowment that will lead to its closing needs a healthy fear.

In my counseling and coaching ministry, I listen to the fears of pastors who suffer from fear. Some see their ministry as insignificant. Some the Spirit of Fear congregations feel that they are inferior. Ministers have the worst crises of limitations. Many pastors feel a call to the ministry is so important that they consider the decision to prepare, go to college and seminary, pass scrutiny by the boards and gatekeepers, and after being in debt, pray that they get a significant call. If the church itself feels insignificant, they cannot support the pastor's fears.

A pastor's fear of messing up often causes her to do just that. She is afraid that if she says the wrong thing or something the powers that be do not like, they will leave the church all upset and blame me. She is usually the last one to hear they left the church. She induces the fear that she cannot make the congregation to be happy. She becomes a people pleaser. The rejection lights up her brain where physical pain originates. There is physical pain when she knows one member, or an entire church is not pleased with her performance.

Inferiority in the ministerial leader's emotional thrust causes secret jealousy of the more successful pastors. Acceptable struggles like overworking or eating too much do not affect how the town or church people see you. They are now broken people. They fear failing. To say to them that the Lord called pastors to be faithful not successful brings a deeper hurt. My brother Edward W. McReynolds has served as a physician in Wilmington, Delaware for more than 50 years. He has served since graduation from the University of Tennessee Medical School.

The fact that some woman or man is reading this book indicates that one is ready to face the fear and to stop hurting. Just being fully aware and that fears could cause your difficulties and struggles. Only when made aware of fears can anyone deal with them.

In identifying fears, a therapist might help you delve into your past and reframe it. The past is gone. None can live with the past. The now is what can be dealt with. One can never create a new past. For our physical, emotional, and spiritual health, we must center ourselves within the present moment. Simply taking time to tap into now will help us relax and to deal with fear in a rational way. Think about what triggers our fears. Learn to put fear in perspective. When we relive those fearful videos inside our brains use cognitive therapy to twist the negative thoughts into positive ones. Most of us focus on thoughts of what could happen. Share thoughts with someone you trust. Paul told us in II Corinthians 10:5, "We take captive every though to make it obedient to Christ."

Journaling or writing down our thoughts about fear is extremely helpful. Write about the exact ways you feel. Writing can help us to become more rational concerning the moments of fear.

In the Spirit of Fear Church, shutting others out, ostracizing them, and rejecting them. There are no exceptions to their rigid rules or criteria for acceptance. Lies and fake stories abound to describe those thought of as inferior or downright inhuman. The safe zone equals the fear zone. There is no grace. Without the grace of God, there is no opening for understanding other people's points of view. They are preoccupied with self-preservation, scarcity, and difficult issues are silenced. In the Spirit of Fear Church, members and the pastor might cite that the Bible teaches obedience on the parts of wives to husbands. A closer reading of the scriptures shows husbands and wives should care for and respect each other. Read Ephesians 5:21-23.

There is little possibility for a Spirit of Fear congregation to step out of its safe zone unless they are aware of how the safe zone works. Fear drives ministers to keep being busy. Some are overly consumed by the fear that by being less vulnerable to criticism in their calling that lay do not comprehend. Some want to feel needed for some mechanistic procedures, certain expected routine, and the fear of lack of purposeful activity. Intense activity acts as a reaction against insecurity. She wants to always be available. That sort of stress brings awareness of her emotional vulnerability, which must be understood as a precondition for any hope of successfully coping with finding balance in living in the face of outrageous assaults that require bring hope in the midst of death, speaking for justice when others are afraid to speak. Some expected to do these things for a lifetime. Grace carries us to a new and right relationship with God which culminates in unconditional love and moments of joy. Environment is always an influence. While sharing the essentials of this book in historic Boston churches, especially the First Baptist Church of Boston. The pastor shared that according to the historic records, his church was the first Baptist congregation in America. The other congregational contenders, Providence and Newport, do not have a church record of their beginnings. In Boston, the Baptists were persecuted severely, especially because of believer's baptism. The state Anglican denomination would allow only infant baptism. Baptists in Boston were treated much like the Anabaptists. Because of this environment, Baptists in Boston met secretly in homes.

One fascinating church in Boston is the Trinity Church. There are giant sculptures of Phillips Brooks inside the sanctuary as well as just outside the massive building. Bostonians held Brooks extremely high in respect and loved his preaching so much they built a church that could hold large crowds. His ministry is lauded even today much like Charles Spurgeon, pastor at the Metropolitan Tabernacle in London. Brooks was a preacher and a pastor. He was recorded as saying, "A preacher who is not a pastor tends to be irrelevant, and a pastor who isn't a preacher tends to get petty." Brooks was reported to have first said of the ministry that our task is to comfort the afflicted and afflict the comfortable. That could well be true, but the task is so difficult in our day when churches never have a permanent more than life sized stature of their minister.

Because clergy represent God in the eyes of a few people, some may come for some type of miraculous divine intervention.

Some parishioners will never be able to change. Day after day, I watch people miss appointments, get drunk again, or hook up with still another abusive partner. I want to cry out in my anger and frustration. People fashion their lives by the choices they make. When people make one bad choice after another, all the church can do is to help them to pick themselves up and start over again

Faith and fear demand that you believe in something you cannot see. You choose.

CHAPTER TWO

The Spirit of Anger Church

Anger has enormous costs to individuals, families, and churches. That impulse that felt so right in the moment, becomes in quiet and storm less days a source for deep regret. That experience that was so worthy of blame passes. The alienation, scars, and hurt remain.

Anger sometimes serves to protect and defend the integrity of a congregation. Chronic anger never makes a church strong or safe. Anger weakens and encourages attack. Anger begets anger. Coping with anger is an active process. Angry people are unwilling to pay the price of letting go. Anger is an ineffective strategy for changing others. In the short term, anger seems to work. If the angry atmosphere continues, those hurt will avoid you. Adapt or let go are the only choices. Two truths that need to be kept in mind are that people change when reinforced to change and they are capable of change. Expecting people or a church to change leads to frustration and disillusions.

One of the most difficult challenges in life is to let go of anger once you have learned to employ it as a defense. The image is that anger is easier to feel than fear or hurt or guilt. All addictions feel better at the moment. Addictions are an avenue to block out pain. Addictions offer a short-term feeling of control and well-being. The aftermath brings the pain. In every situation except direct threats, anger leads away from appropriate action. Anger keeps us from fixing anything. Deep frustrations bring stuck feelings masked by anger.

Chronically angry people destroy relationships. Anger brings insensitivity to pain and pleasure. Anger kills love and the warmth and touch of love. Anger brings coldness, withdrawal, and more anger in return.

Stress is the fuel for anger. Angry people must learn how to reduce stress. Learn to relax. Go to a quiet place. Be in a comfortable position. Feel your emotions here and now. A candle flame or soft music is helpful.

When coping strategies fail, a growing sense of helplessness fills your soul. Problems appear to have no solution. The result is chronic emotional pain. Use a journal to pinpoint where to pay attention. Areas for examination include health problems, financial stress, work-related issues, living situations, or interpersonal relationship issues, family troubles, or psychological issues including excessive anxiety such as being obsessed with unattainable goals or lack of motivation or faith.

Anger is not an emotion that happens in a flash. Even people who are "quick to anger" or who are described as one with a "short fuse" With irritation the fires of anger become flamed and fanned, the body tenses up. Confronted with incongruent ambiguous thoughts, the videos of past hurts begin to play. Who or what in the past caused you pain? The process of comparing the present situation to past experience is unconscious so there is no thought of doing this process. A church leader or a pastor may have been a source of spiritual or other abuse. She has the same physical characteristics with similar gestures, body language, facial expression, and tone of voice. Present relationships are contaminated from past ones. Escalation is not inevitable. Ineffective behavior is influenced by attitude. Human action when angry has much to do with the attitude toward conflict. The worst kind of attitude is thinking pain must be paid back. They seek retribution and they want "an eye for an eye." The conflict never stops. Intimidated, frightened people that are pushed around find other methods of getting back at those with whom they are angry.

Whenever I lead anger management therapy groups, I begin with this quotation from Aristotle from *The Nicomachean Ethics*. "Anyone can become angry—that is easy. But to be angry with the right person, to the right degree, at the right time, for the right purpose, and in the right way . . . this is not easy."

Anger is the least socially acceptable emotion. Anger is tremendous energy propelled by the thought of attack. When we are not safe with our hurt and fear, which is underneath our anger. Anger is the survival emotion. We think, "Kill or be killed." People are out to get us. Anger decreases love in our relationships. From generation to generation, our families have been uncomfortable with anger. Our inner souls become numb. We feel ice cold to those who we love. Sharing our hurt helps us see anger as a wall to protect ourselves. Suppressing anger will draw angry people to us.

During court required angel management counseling, I ask, "Somebody give me a definition of anger." Most clients do not know what anger is. So then I ask them, "Can you give me a word that you associate with the emotion anger?"

With a frown and glazed eyes, a woman yelled, "Rage." A man said, "Putting the hurt on people." Another charged with domestic violence said, "Losing my control." When I tell them anger is a normal human emotion, I joy in the looks on their confused as some heard this for the first time. I then read from a dictionary, "A feeling one has toward something that offends, opposes, or annoys."

One of my clients presented an anonymous rhyme about anger: "When I have lost my temper

I have lost my reason too.

I'm never proud of anything

Which angrily I do.

When I have talked in anger

And my cheeks wee flaming red,

I have always uttered something

Which I wish I had not said.

In anger I have never

Done a kindly deed or wise,

But many things for which I felt

I should apologize.

In looking back across my life,

And all I've lost or made,

I can't recall a single time

When my rage ever paid.

So I struggle to be patient,

For I've reached a wiser age;

I do not want to do a thing

Or speak a word in rage.

I have learned by sad experience

That when my temper flies

I never do a worthy deed,

A decent deed or wise.

Internal questions I ask are "What must be protected? What must be restored?" Symptoms include apathy, depression, boundary loss, hatred, prejudice, enmeshment, self-abandonment, and isolation.

People who are not able to communicate assertively are usually angry. Their anger results from not being able to ask for what they want. They desire to protect themselves by setting limits, not being able to motivate others to negotiate or cooperate. They may silently blame instead of listening. Teaching church groups to be assertive will eliminate anger-generating situations.

Anger sets boundaries by looking into your soul's perimeter and keeping an eye on you and your environment. When boundaries are broken by insensitivity or jealousy, anger restores your strength and separateness. So then you can speak and act out of your strength, rather than passivity or brutality. Repressing that anger causes people to lose the energy to protect themselves from soulful damage. That damage comes from unskilled and terrible uses of anger when it comes.

When anger is not allowed its natural flow, boundaries will not be maintained and your love for yourself will cause reliance on the opinions of the outside world.

Among the healing thoughts we can share, these are helpful. It is safe to express anger. It's human to get angry. I can take no for an answer. Anger is a harmless emotion. I can express anger appropriately. I have no need to separate myself when I am angry. People will love and accept me even when I am angry.

All emotions travel in pairs or in groups and are connected. Sometimes the Spirit of Fear Church cannot be distinguished from the Spirit of Anger Church. Both project from power struggles or enmeshment. We must learn to channel anger as we gain self-control, wisdom, clarity, capacity for mercy, and the ability to rise from any fall.

Healthy anger is a decisive and self-defining emotion. Anger exists to protect you, your moral structure, and people around you. Anger and healthy boundaries are intimately connected. The Spirit of Anger Church has trouble with boundaries.

Unresolved or repressed anger destroys marriages, families, communities, as well as churches. The root cause of a spirit of anger is tension from present or past hurts, fear, and guilt.

Rejection and anger are strong factors in life. As a child, we form attachments with parents, friends, relatives, and community groups. We feel security from each of them. When those who are trusted communicate rejection, the secure world collapses. And the fears come galloping in bringing deep bitterness toward anyone responsible for her pain. Accepting unchangeable features such as physical appearance, birth order, race, mental abilities, or family can be difficult. One who experiences rejection will be extremely sensitive to those who ridicule.

Anger comes as a reaction to favoritism. Rejection comes from a call to a church, a divorce, a job, apathy, or the anguish of false accusations. A false accusation not only damages the one accused, but it stirs up indignation and a desire to see the false accuser brought to justice.

Fear, guilt, anger, and anxiety surrounds the memory of these experiences that brought deep hurt.

People who represent another group, another religion, or another race come within crosshairs of projection of the misbehavior of one to the entire group. That's where hate comes. These generalizations are often part of the Spirit of Anger Church. Ephesians 4:31-32 speaks to the church. "Let all bitterness, and wrath, and anger, and clamor, and evil speaking, be put away from you, with all malice: and be ye kind one to another, even as God for Christ's sake hath forgiven you."

The Spirit of Anger Church tends to call a woman or man filled with unresolved anger. Any minister holding on or repressing unresolved anger is like a time bomb bringing damage. Often, she comes divorced, defensive, thin-skinned, beating up her sheep instead of feeding them, preaching that is graceless, blaming others for her failures, driving healthy people from the church.

Church members bring unresolved anger into the congregation. Some may be leaders in the church. When those angry people are the ministers or spiritual leaders, nothing but negativity will take place.

The angry minister wants people to fear her. She is blunt. Intimidation is a tool that is used. Coercion and manipulation help enable the conquest.

A Presbyterian pastor was approached by one of her members with this advice: "Pastor, the world and my job environment beat the hell out of me. I don't need you to do the same thing when you preach on Sunday mornings."

People who attend church want to be inspired and encouraged by being in worship. They come seeking hope and a joyful atmosphere. She just talked about the agenda for women or the denomination's overall plan to set people straight.

Remember my questions used in anger management: What must be protected? What must be restored?

When a congregation or an individual solves the conflict, they have to focus and reground, burn some unhealthy contracts, and thus rejuvenating the environment. Anger is an emotion containing incredible energy into a human system. One is now a different person. "The joy of the Lord" is now the strength. You and your congregation can now rejoice in that resolved anger is now a boundary setter, a conflict mediator, and protector of the peace that passes all understanding. Silently repeat, "What needs to be protected? What needs to be restored?" Healthy anger, like every emotion, arrives inside, addresses an issue, then moves on.

Anger is listed as one of the seven deadly sins. The other six are sloth and avarice, pride and envy, lust and gluttony. Those are best understood within the eye of anger. Some label pride the most deadly sin. Pride causes humans to see themselves as greater than they are. Proverbs in the Old Testament declares, "Pride goeth before a fall." The proud are angry at anyone who challenges them. Tyrants become angry at their people. Celebrities get angry at their fans. Some ministers get angry with church members.

Envy has the same proportions and the same symptoms of rage. The proud imagine others faring better than them. They conclude that the whole world is unjust and particularly unjust to them. Some views in and pleasure intertwined together.

Lust and gluttony are sensuality based. The lustful think lust is a human need. The lusty failing to receive pleasure give in to rage. The language of smuts the language of lust. The words include violence. There is a church that began in Lincoln, Nebraska called the Church of Fuck Yeah. God help us.

In writing of gluttony, Paul refers to people "whose god is their belly. "Some churches in the South find a vital need to have an eating shelter on the campus of the church. Folks suffering from major depression tend to eat too much and use food as a way to cope.

Avarice and sloth come in opposite poles of human activity. It's the coach potato over against the go-getter.

The sloths try to remain as passive as possible. Millions sit like dead people in front of their televisions.

Avarice people desire to become prosperous with money and things. The love of money is the root of all evil. The ultimate aim of all evil is sin, which is death. Anger keeps company with all the deadly sins. Uncontrolled anger distorts the sense of self and the world. She has eaten and digested the forbidden fruit that she perceives will change her into a god.

Anger is not just an uncontrollable impulse. Some abusive spouses relate how they "lost it." He lost control and has no sense of the harm done. The people of the Spirit of Anger Church say, "For that moment, he just was not his real self." Anger and blame march along together. They are the fire and the flame. Blame enables anger. Sometimes angry abusers blame the victim of injustice to keep calm. They cast the first stone. Blame was in the story of Adam and Eve. Sometimes in marriage counseling sessions, therapists or pastors might say, "Neither of you is completely to blame, but both are responsible."

In families many children are traumatized by the anger of their parents. Even as adults these children feel helpless and intimidated by anger. Children learn to be angry from the parents. Someone coming from an unhealthy angry home will find it difficult to relate in a marriage if the spouse did not experience the angry atmosphere of home.

As a psychiatric therapist, I often observed that in psychotic cases, children have learned to be angry from adults. Even if a child relearns how to do anger and resolves to be calmer than her parents, she continues to shape herself too.

An angry family is one in which the parents set a toxic example by being angry much of the time. They teach by their example that anger brings power. Parents must work on their own emotional reactions before they can expect the children to change.

Some church families echo the indulgent family who desires peace at any price. Anger does not pay. Parents must discipline and thus save a lot of time and effort that will be required. Today's children and youth have schedules that lead to stress. Each member of the family goes in different directions for music lessons, basketball, football, wrestling, with no letup the overbooked parents and the children create a trigger for anger.

In the book of James 1:26, we read: "If anyone thinks he is religious and does not bridle his tongue but deceives his heart, this man's religion is vain." Explosive anger is not a way to become a kingdom person. Those who persist in angry explosions cannot be anything but miserable. During childhood some learn to be angry because they find they can control others by exploding in rage. That's just learned manipulation and it is self-defeating. Some children are frustrated with the treatment they received in their home. They kept seeing their parents go wild when anger exploded, and the children copy that behavior. They are not aware that they have a choice. They hold on to the angry blowups throughout their lives. If we choose to have a different response to this emotion, we begin to live more and more in an environment of joy and peace.

Within the church or in a therapist's office, I often quote the Bible: "Fathers, provoke not your children to wrath." Never play on your children's guilt. Manipulations of conscience cause the grown-up child to feel eight years old again. Older adults need to learn to live in the moment, the now. Youth need to realize that a moment only lasts today.

"Unless you become as a child, you shall not enter the kingdom of God. "Childlike faith casts out our rage. An atmosphere of anger causes us to continue to come apart like we did in our pointless rebellion, the temper shows, the withdrawals and other terrifying experiences. Only now, my corporate attorney young daughter have I realized how my anger touched her in childhood. When women reach middle age, most grow in wisdom, grace, and love. Men can also gain that wisdom as they admit the good sense, strength, and competence of the women in their lives.

Angry men need angry women who communicate wisdom to their middle age daughters. Women are better coping with anger than men. In society we assume that women will repress their rage. Men and women must understand that life is full of opportunities to make decisions, even though most decisions are made for us. We hunger for limitless self-determination that will be undercut by the common experience of powerlessness.

Pathological stuff is found inside the church. In 65 years as a minister, I have noticed the pathology firsthand. In my retirement time, among my many interests, I am planting a church called the Spirit of Joy Church. Most of my members have been hurt by churches or are the type of people not welcomed such as addicts, seekers, thinkers, or grateful refugees from some other congregations who do not attend any church. We all share horrible stories. How does a church become such a dangerous and unhappy place? Church people should ooze out love, but the feelings of anger, guilt, fear, hate, jealousy, and exclusion prevail in most. Any national or state assembly of church leaders holds to a vocabulary of code where nobody says exactly what she means. I experienced this as I served as moderator in a Christian Church (Disciples of Christ) Region. Pastors with frozen and repressed feelings say what they think they are supposed to feel instead of what they really feel. Sickness in the church derives from incomplete digestion of the power within the congregations that counts "powers and principalities" as works of darkness.

Christianity needs leaders who are vulnerable. To be present in the moment is vital in making tough decisions for the long-term health of the church. The energy of anger requires pastors to lead from the heart with compassion. We cannot hide. Effective ministers demonstrate vulnerability and transparency with humility. Leading the Spirit of Anger Church requires self-awareness, the ability to look inward with honesty about what we are feeling. The church needs women and men of courage to create an environment by being still, open to change and to be aware of the centering when doing ministry. We can never be perfect. We must celebrate our imperfections. Be open about mistakes or when we miss the mark. Somehow, the anger energy removes the walls that have built up over time. This new wave of energy creates comfort, better communication, and authenticity. God calls and helps the group do something outside the walls.

Vulnerability is such a rich word. It continues to be misinterpreted. It means talking about your emotions, asking for what is needed, showing up and being seen, or having difficult and painful conversations. Vulnerability is not an experience we run towards. There is a spiritual mystery hidden within it to give motivation to experience it. To love like Jesus is to be vulnerable. As we take this leap of faith, we risk being hurt or rejected. Whole hearted living in Christ is about engaging with life from a place of worthiness. Vulnerability is at the center of moments of joy, fear, shame, sorrow, disappointment, belonging, creativity, and gratitude. When we are asked, "Who is great?" only a few would point to people who are merely great at something. Greatness goes beyond our looks, our talents, our intellect and our skills.

Jesus said, "You know that among the Gentiles those whom they recognize as their rulers lord it over them, and their great ones are tyrants over them. But it is not so among you; but whoever wishes to become great among you must be your servant, and whoever wishes to be first among you must be slave of all." Some people become ordained because they felt little love as they grew up. They look for the church to give them a life. Clergy persons experience the anger of those in their parishes. When ministers meet in support groups or in blogs, the ones who are being crucified sound like celebrities or CEOs. Powerful people in the church denounce the pastor who was the predecessor. They lament over her incompetence. It is wise to remember to love those who served before us as we love ourselves. They will certainly react the same when you leave. With a new church call, people will say, "You are like fresh air to our church." Those same people will vote in anger to get you doomed and crucified.

The after a pastor leaves congregation, sometimes the anger is expected. This happens when an abuse of power comes in ways such as financial or sexual misconduct has occurred. Boundaries and expectations have been violated. The church becomes a Spirit of Anger Church and they must reestablish new boundaries. Expectations and trust have to be renegotiated. The church may be loyal to a charismatic, talented minister of 40 years rather than believe her accusers. Anger is a warning sign that the church is in trouble.

Anger is never a private feeling. Sometimes the angry group are angry about situations they care about. Those people all are in connection. The fury happens because the expectations were not fulfilled. This evasion of feeling spreads widely in the community.

Sometimes people in the congregation throw their anger at God. When we use angry profane words, we are stressed. Irritation with God is found throughout

Christian history. The Book of Job asks should we praise God for blessings, but never complain about bad or negative events. There will be degrees of anger at God and the church. Religion with all its rules and constraints brings anger to the soul. One of my clients left a strict fundamentalist congregation. He took his family with him to attend a progressive United Methodist Church. He felt shame and guilt. The insufferable restraints had led him into depression. His persistent depression was a symptom that he was now living contrary to his faith. Find the angriest lawyers in a dysfunctional law firm. Some of them should not have chosen to be lawyers. Most of these attorneys cannot imagine being anything else. My client dealt with the depression by finding a place that was a joy to his soul.

Even in a Spirit of Joy Church, members will be required to understand and live with anger, as well as fear, anxiety, and guilt. In the Sermon on the Mount, Jesus gives a hard saying. Jesus said, "I say to you that everyone who is angry with his brother will be liable to judgment." The Scriptures affirm that anger is sometimes right and needs to be felt. God is also angry. And God is love. Sin is a constant danger when anger is felt. Paul wrote, "Be angry but do not sin; do not let the sun go down on your anger, and do not make room for the devil." Humans often distort their sense of justice. Little things anger them. Psychologists observe that people who cannot feel angry are defective. There is a condemnation in anger that involves illusory self-perceptions. Angry people look down in judgment on that person who hurt her. They think that they are better than other sinners. It is not a surprise that the early church regarded anger as one of the seven deadly sins. Uncontrolled anger kills love and everything lovely.

Colossians 3:8 guides us to "get rid" of anger. Most anger is not righteous. The Spirit of Joy Church enables believers to get rid of it. Eliminating inappropriate anger is a spiritual goal. We must find the way to rise above the anger. Anger involves unrealistic expectations, inflated sense of our importance, attachments to worldly goods, and a misdirected passion for justice. Ministering to one another includes repentance and a desire to change.

Journaling our episodes of anger helps us see if the anger was justified. We must lean on the Spirit of God to get rid of anger and to put on kindness, humility, gentleness, patience, forgiveness, gratitude, love and peace. The Spirit of Joy Church guides the furious to avoid the bulging eyes, racing heart rate, flushing face, raising voice, and aggressive gestures, replacing them with spiritual virtues that aim toward the goal of not doing inappropriate anger.

Prayer is a way to change perception. Prayer helps us reconcile so as not to break the relationship with God and others. Compassionate prayer will enable the Spirit of Anger Church to become a Spirit of Joy Church. The joy of the Lord is our strength. Charles Spurgeon, the prince of preachers, told his London congregation, "Anxiety does not empty tomorrow of its sorrows, but only empties today of its strengths." Anxiety is a spiritual question about redeeming the anxiety within. "In this world you will have tribulation," said Jesus. He spoke of his anxiety and his earthly journey that will result in death. In Jesus' anxious prayer in Gethsemane reveals his fear of separation and being forsaken by God.

The Spirit of Anxiety churches become locked into misguided interpretation or the lack of joy in life. The church becomes a prison for dread and confusion, spiritual disability, and lack of faith. My own vision for "creating an atmosphere where joy and miracles happen," and in that environment our future is bright. The environment of a community of faith is never about just socializing but is a gift from God. Life in spiritual gatherings is observed, felt, and expressed in the ties that bind in relationships. The joy of the Lord comes from participation in a faith community in which we believe and live by faith.

Dr. Wayne Oates taught at the University of Louisville Medical School as well as the Southern Baptist Theological Seminary, said, "This drive toward community transforms anxiety into a social feeling. The church converts egocentric anxieties into a fellowship of concern for other people."

To protect against idolatry, we must create that atmosphere where our love of people includes neighbor love, recognizing and loving the image of God in them, and only then can we love them as a friend. The church family is free of idolization of both the people we love and our love itself by learning to love God most of all. The church must depend on the Holy Spirit for the power to "lead a life worthy of the calling to which we have been called, with all humility and gentleness, with patience, bearing one another in love."

In I Corinthians 12, Paul writes a letter requesting unity in the Corinth church. A woman finds a bottle on the beach. Out pops a genie who says one wish would be granted to her. She says, "I just wish for world peace, especially in my own country." The genie looked at her and told her that her wish was one even beyond genie power. Do you have another wish? She said, "Well how about peace in the church where I serve as the pastor?" The genie replied, "Now, what was your first wish?"

The Christian servant biggest work hazard is discouragement. Spirit of anger congregations give little support, love, or joy in being its pastor. Eventually, with all the churches, we will receive an appointment or calling to a negative focused church. The truth is not "if" we will find frustration, but "when" we find a need just to persevere.

We simply must expect these dry seasons with doubts and confusion. And in those most difficult places, we must depend on our faith, especially when we don't feel like it. We live as if in a heavy winter fog. That blinding mist feels like the only possible reality. The colors are gray, the air is heavy, and the goal is out of sight. Nothing lifts the emotional mood.

Being discouraged in a crappy situation is not a sin. Suppress those emotions by pretending everything is fine leads to sickness and unhealthy reactions. Chad Stoner, pastor of the Stony Brook Church in Omaha, shared a three days Winter Convocation on "Yes to the Mess." He told the gathered pastors that we could tell God that this ministry sucks. Healing comes from raw honesty in venting about our most selfish feelings. Lean in completely broken with the full weight of the burden."

To live through an atmosphere filled the energies of anger, as well other difficult feelings. We need to discover a permanent affirming encouragement that does not change with our current surroundings. Friends and support groups can help, but they cannot become the constancy we need. Christ Jesus brings people together in the kingdom of God. Some of my most helpful friends are people whom I could never had met on my own. We need some serious deep fellowship to get through the fog of the hardest seasons.

With the joy of the Lord as our strength, we make a bigger impact than we think. We can then accept the highs and lows in ministry that are mountain high glorious and lonesome valley deep. If we expect applause from the congregation, forget that ole dream. Seasoned ministers expect resistance as we use our gifts. We might experience not much fruit, but we keep on planting seeds. God is not done with us yet.

I have been led to write this book with the colored lenses on my own experiences, personal perceptions failures and successes. I claim only to be a fellow practitioner who owns and affirms both the mess and the joy of ministry. I have attempted to touch base with the real struggles in ministry by using first person experiences, both my own and others. My effort will enable us toward a healthy combination of positive regard for ourselves and an awareness of the limits.

We might feel that God is done with us. We may perceive that we have been brutalized by the institutional church. To be authentic we must support these who have been serving in bad times. Some might feel called to regional or conference leadership to be a genuine supporter of all the pastors and churches in their areas of care. Ministers struggle each day for a greater sense of self-determination. They free themselves from the prison of an inadequate self-image. Few ministers have systematically tried to teach their congregations what ministers do. Some may think they know how the pastor functions. Their knowledge comes from tradition and media, which is mostly incomplete and inaccurate. People could be invited to come to the pastor's home to learn about her work. Most members of churches operate around conceptions that are decades old. Churches must be updated frequently as to the work of a church leader. Pastors suffer intense stress, much of it comes from the fact that the membership has little awareness of what she actually does. In some places the lay members come to realize that their concepts were outdated. People have a deep need to love and to be loved and the need to be aware that they are worthwhile to themselves and to others. These steps will bring more affirmation and appreciation from the church body, instead of the predictable burnout.

The presence of stress is not the problem. The problem is the church has not come to understanding the sources and solutions to the stress of ministry. Not every minister finds the stress to be overwhelming. She must become aware of their work so she can accept their place and get more control over the ambiguities relating to her service. If not, coping will be impossible.

Humans can take our ministries away. They cannot take your calling from God. To continue to be alive in an oasis in the desert, we must let the "joy of the Lord" be our strength so we can keep ministering to the pasture when powers and authorities put us out to pasture. Jesus' joy gives us kingdom peace even when we feel emotionally in the depths of paralysis. Thousands have their ministry taken away. A low percentage of seminary graduates receive a call as a pastor. Why are there more seminaries than the church will ever need? There are churches that change pastors every year. Pastors experience the loss of love, support, and respect because of the "agents of the prince of this world."

The abuse of power happens in politics, workplaces, as well as in the churches. Any professing member of a congregation, including the pastor, can abuse power. We permit positions and power to block the way of humility and obedience. Rumors spread rapidly in the right environment.

One time an elected leader with power over ministers was found to be a cross dresser as he bought women's clothing in a store. At first the manager thought that these were for his wife, but he bought so much that gossip accused him of cross dressing. When the proud person was found out, he began to cause trouble for those who knew. He was living opposite lives in and out of the church. It is so frustrating when people have one church face and another community face.

They may shout "amen" at a clergy gathering. Their actions outside the walls of the church they expose out themselves otherwise. Their angry abuse of power comes from their anxiety, fear, and guilt.

Vulnerability is a deep sacred place. Every church leader will find it a venture that is a necessary. It is messy. It hurts. Those who have served as pastor of two or more congregations will eventually experience opening up to the wrong person. We let them in, and we are betrayed. Most react by keeping people at a distance. We live in fear of more rejections. We then doubt if it's ever worth it to pour ourselves out for another.

Offending people come into church with many scars. Ministry will involve blame and responsibility, mental health issues, anger management, scars from childhood, powerlessness, and trust problems. Only a healthy church can help him reclaim his life. She or he probably had anger management courses while in prison. Some offenders have mental health problems that go far beyond what a pastor or her congregation is competent to handle. A referral is the best source. The responsibility for healing is the responsibility of the offender.

Paul wrote in II Corinthians 12:10 that he was content with his weaknesses, insults, hardships, persecutions, and calamities. For when I am weak, then I am strong.

When we share our weaknesses, we show our humanity. God's strength is made perfect in weakness. When we have the courage to be authentic, people will take notice. Emotionally hurting people crave authenticity as a wonderful conduit where grace abounds.

Anger is a big part in the hurts that were never healed. Those videos of anguish and pain keep playing over and over in our minds. Healing comes as we get in touch with the emotion resulting from the hurt. Have a coach or spiritual director redirect the anger at yourself for allowing this tragic wound to keep you from living a productive, joy-filled and anger-free life. The worst thing we can do is to keep being in denial how deeply those scars are inside. Healing of memories is beyond any blessing. We find peace with our past by forgiving those who dealt the harm. Healing memories will cause us to become our very best selves that God created us to be.

We hold the misconception that weakness must be avoided. In reality our tendency to show anger or other emotions has to be embraced. Our lives and the lives of others can be restored by the power of the Holy Spirit. When we successfully deal with those vulnerable times, God is glorified, and the ministry thrives. Joy and miracles are born in the vulnerable encounters. Those we serve will made a connection when we open up to share our struggles, lessons, and trials, people will find hope in their own situations.

In my ten and a half years as pastor for the First Christian Church in Weeping Water, I taught the Psalms for about four years on Wednesday nights with the prayer meetings. Some of the Psalms appeared to protest God with expressions of anger and fear. We all believed that the Psalms were God's Word given to enable our prayer lives. Since we tackled all 150 Psalms, we ran into the psalms of lament.

We discovered we could pray the psalms that were not focused on praise or thanksgiving, or even confession. This congregation possessed a high view of the Bible as the Word of God. We found that we had been cherry-picking our studies reading some preferred verses. With my Hebrew Bible from seminary, we did not skip the difficult psalms. We attempted to pray as wide and deep as these psalms led us. Two problems that might come up include deciding if it is real or sound, acceptable to bring before God the negative sentiments that most of us had avoided all our lives. And also, is it acceptable to be angry with God?

Ours was not a church with a spirit of anger. Still these laments expressing hopelessness, anger, and pain. If we only study the "happy" psalms, and skip the negative psalms, we are missing out on a gift of the Spirit of God that is God's desire. The Psalter draws us to ponder the hopes, cares, perplexities, doubts, griefs, sorrows, fears, and all the distracting emotions and experiences that we avoid. Joy and encouragement are vital, but we believe God wants us to address all of life's emotions, bringing them all before the God of life. The joy of the Lord as our strength is needed, but this reliance on joy can be exhausted, and even cynical.

Some people have even left the church because they were experiencing fear, anger, and hopelessness, but these were never addressed. They are thrown into a deep worry and confusion as some church leaders expound that it is a great sin to be angry with God. Like in the case of the life of Job, God choices to permit Satan to hurt Job and his family. Exodus and Numbers gives multitudes of stories of the grumbling Israelites after they had been miraculously delivered from slavery in Egypt. They turned away from God. In their anger, they berated Moses. They then started worship of a golden calf. When we are angry with God, we wallow in self-pity and serve other gods.

Some congregations teach that expressing anger at God is a sign of unfaithfulness. On the cross Jesus quoted the psalmist words, "Why have you forsaken me?" Jesus was not controlled by fear that his question of protest would offend his Father. When we feel abandoned by God, we can call out, "My God, my God." The Spirit laments in us as we call out to the Father. Unlike Jesus in his earthly ministry, we act as if we can ignore more than a third of the Psalms.

Our four-year study taught us that in addition to psalms of praise and joy, thanksgiving and confession, our covenant with God calls us to bring in prayer our hopelessness, bitterness, and anger before God. We trust God as wrestle with God's promises. Most of us become angry with God when things go wrong. God permits bad things to happen in our lives. Some call this God's permissive will. His will is not for terrible things to happen to us. God's thoughts are not our thoughts. Everything that happens is for some greater good. The Psalms focus on the eternal good that matters, and that is impossible for us to figure out. We find biblical evidence that it is permissible to be frustrated at God. God is not to blame.

We think we can manipulate God with our prayers. We think if we pray hard enough, we think our Lord must provide whatever we ask. We can't take no for an answer. Jesus taught us to pray, "Thy will be done." If we stay angry with God, we show a lack of knowledge of God. The more we know God, the less likely we will be angry with God.

God is love, and we need to praise out of our intuitive knowledge of his goodness. Paul said in the immortal Romans 8:28, "We know that in everything God works for good with those who love him, who are called according to his purpose." With grace, we seek God's help in curbing our anger. We must bring kindness, forgiveness, and joy into the deepest parts of our being. We will not show mildness to others if our hearts are churning with harshness. When we fail to accomplish our spiritual goal of staying calm, we can review what happened and find the strength to determine how not to fail in the future. This will constantly remind us of the benefits to be gained. Harming ourselves and others will be avoided. Write in a journal the negative results of continuing to explode and read it with prayers every day. Members of our churches and families enable by those who help you do what you are struggling not to do. Spending too much time in an angry atmosphere is asking for trouble.

Our courage to go deeper in the Scriptures gives us insight into handling our own anger so that we can grow more into our identity with Christ. Willpower alone will not help. Overcoming anger is worth striving toward, so that we can live with love, joy, and grace.

CHAPTER THREE

The Spirit of Anxiety Church

Anxieties come in many shapes with various amounts of intensity. Every person has them. We fear that we will be hurt, made to suffer pain, loss, harassment, embarrassment, inconveniences, or things we think are bad. These fears condition the response to living in many ways, limiting us and limiting what God can do through us.

We do not always know why we have the jitters. For no apparent reason, nervousness overwhelms. At times people know exactly what they are afraid. Anxiety is fear that we will die. We are not likely to drop dead from anxiety. If we could live without any stress or anxiety, that life would be without challenge. Christians and congregations fear that they are failing God. Nobody can be bold and fearless at all times. Even Jesus sweat blood in anticipation of the cross. Some avoid church and avoid interactions with members of the congregation. They may have expressed anger inappropriately. So they seal off in the comfort of their home. Avoidance seems natural to those using the strategy of avoidance is common. One of my clients grew so anxious that he was painfully uncomfortable during church services. So he just stayed home. Those tempted to avoid situations that cause anxiety might be directed to study the consequences of that habit.

Anxiety elicited by certain others is so disturbing that they avoid the church fellowship and the people. They go to elaborate lengths to avoid meeting such people. Others are afraid of saying the wrong thing. They could be extreme introverts who feel extraverts pull their life energy in the group cluster.

Those with a social anxiety disorder are facing an intense fear or anxiety of being judged, negatively evaluated, or rejected in a social situation. Social anxiety strikes wherever groups gather, large or small, without any reason. This happens in an unorganized crowd such as an outdoor meeting on a college campus.

Because of the mental health stigma, some people refuse to talk about it. In a heavily extroverted society, people become obsessed with being friendly and charming, outgoing, but anxiety clashes with all that.

Some exuberant religious people advise to fake it until you make it, or they'll just say, "Just get over it." With that kind of environment, millions are misunderstood and blame themselves for their reactions. They hate not sharing the joy like the normal people. Unless the church shares the good news about social anxiety, they suffer in silence. They withdraw more and more, which causes things to be worse.

Stress and anxiety affect our lives in differing ways. Two thirds of office visits to physicians are prompted by stress related symptoms. Anxiety affects emotional, spiritual, and physical living.

Some stress is positive. The pressure to complete writing a book serves as motivation and encouragement to spend hours in front of a computer screen. Without some stress, this project would never have been completed.

Stress and anxiety can get out of our control. We are limited with this crippling emotion and we respond in inappropriate ways. Our bodies slowly destroy themselves. Anxiety gnaws at the essence of our being. As I got older, my body began to become weak. My muscles had no tone. My doctor prescribed physical therapy to make repairs and to give me more strength.

The ways some try to cope with stress are ineffective. These searches for answers demand our energy and cause us to worry about things other than those that bring us abundant life. The Spirit of Anxiety Church focuses on the bottom line, or sheer numbers, emphasizing quantity over quality. Money and size are the goals that bring darkness and anxiety.

Faith is telling ourselves the truth about God and ourselves and our situation. In the New Testament, James wrote that faith always includes action. We must tell ourselves the truth and resolve to being by "doing" what we avoid because of the emotions. Conquering anxiety comes from faithfully telling the truth and doing that which exposes us to the fear-filled atmospheres we have attempted to avoid. No condition is hopeless. We can evaluate why things we have tried have not brought help. We keep on to finally find a solution. God will never leave us in our difficulties. The Word of God says that God loves every one of us. The promise is that we can cast our cares on our Lord.

Jesus taught that a faithful life is the best stress and anxiety reducer. In Matthew 5-7, Jesus gives the importance of putting faith in God above anything else. Our vulnerable lives must be primarily and totally devoted to God alone. My first sermon was from Matthew 6:33, "Seek ye first the kingdom of God, and all these things will be added unto you."

Charles Spurgeon lived with anxiety and stress. He suffered crippling depression that led to his death in his early 50's. Most of the time he suffered in secret, all alone. Jesus gave us the radical challenge to reorient or lives toward humility and obedience. As we do this, the things that once claimed our anxious attention fade from importance. The tension to thrive and survive leaves. Anxiety causes confusion about being and doing. We get terribly concerned about what we will be doing. God cares more about who we are and how we are.

We who exist in the kingdom of God never know a person's real problems, and we are not the professionals that bring solutions. The children of God care and let others care for them. Bringing in the joy of the Lord requires us to keep a safe distance from those we are called to serve. Laying down our lives means living our own faith and doubts, joys and sadness, courage and fear, and hope and despair in the midst of struggles who are getting in touch with the Lord of life. The reality is that we are sinful, broken people who need care and much as those for whom we care. The essence of serving as a pastor begs for redefinition.

The only minister to serve the Spirit of Anxiety Church would be one who has a non-anxious presence as she lives within the anxiety of the people, she is called to serve. Anxiety cannot be avoided. Just being a group of gathered humans inevitably brings anxiety. Anxiety is as infectious as the flu. We give it to others, and they give it to us. The emotional pain of anxiety constricts freedom to move in the Spirit bringing uncertainty. It also limits creativity. In my experience anxiety arises with loss of a pastor, a new building program, loss or gain of members, or money problems. Putting anxiety to rest is difficult. Anxious people are sensitive to everything. They are easily hurt. Reasoning with those who are clinically anxious will not help. It becomes a disorder and they cannot escape the bondage of being locked in and stuck. To conquer anxiety people may need professional help. Those using therapy will find a way to regain the joy.

The DSM IV label, Generalized Anxiety Disorder, is how clients are described in the clinic and is common. Anxiety is the feeling of a sense of dread, nervousness, apprehension, or leaving one's own home. Anxiety arrives when we must make an important decision. Ill health brings on anxiety. Safety for family and friends, finances, and life in general are keys to anxiety. If we reject all emotions, we will cycle into worry as fears of the unknown. With nothing to hold to, there remains a nagging feeling of distress. A key to therapy is to focus and take time to sort out perceptions. Anxiety prepares people to face what is not happening now, but really could take place at a future time.

Some psychiatric therapists argue with clients. I have used these after a time of talking to help them to become convinced of the truth and that truth will take hold in their souls and minds. Engaging with the therapist helps people imitate and assimilate the strategies to use in arguing down misbeliefs, making room for the truth to take root and grow.

Our life journeys involve the reality of irritations, annoyances and crisis. The journey is a struggle which the Scriptures call a battle. The Bible tells us that nobody can travel through life without disappointment, rejection, pain, mistakes, loneliness, and emotional anguish.

We never can get enough of the emotional benefits of joy. Still it is a painful puzzle learning to live with anxiety. Nobody has come to me as a pastor or therapist to get rid of joy.

Worry prevents us to climb into higher happiness because it prevents living in the present. We tend to think about what will happen. Our predictions are negative, defeatist thoughts like predictions of extreme worriers.

Some descriptions heard during therapy include, "People think I am just overreacting." Others tell them it's no big deal. "Instead of mocking me, just show some empathy, some words of encouragement." Kind words of encouragement will go a long way. One client said, "I wish I could tell more people about my social anxiety, but I worry that I am some weak woman with a mental illness. "Anxious people sometimes talk too fast because they are uncomfortable trying to get through interactions to spare themselves the pain. Trying to use force to help them communicate will not help. Anxiety feels like being persecuted just because you are who you are.

Anxiety is not always linked to physical danger. Grounding and calming your tension are methods for focusing so we can feel safe. The church could offer or refer members to tai chi, yoga walking in nature which helps restore balance. Anxiety must be faced with action. The most unrecognized and unexamined aspect of the problem is avoidance. Avoidance is the reason problems with anxiety yield no action. The very actions that many choose are the cause of complicating worries

Desensitization and cognitive reframing methods can bring the intellect into the healing. Also, calming movement is better than stillness for anxiety-filled people. Our personal space will welcome healthy energy for restoration. Anxiety causes troubles as it feels trapped in your body. If we can get it out and talk about it, we have access to unlimited intuition and information. When families or congregations are stuck or confused, therapy can help track their fearful and anxious paths to help the action to heal.

There is more than one way to perceive most anything. We are all anxious in that each member of the body of Christ has a different point of view based on a myriad of thoughts, experiences, and emotions. Often, we must not forget or refuse to look beyond our own perception.

Church leaders are totally exposed. They live in a torture chamber of uncertainty. They must take a huge emotional risk where we open ourselves to vulnerability. Most leaders are willing to share behind their walls. Few are willing to show up in their brokenness so that all glory goes to God.

Far from being a protective shield, the illusion of invulnerability undermines that very response that would have given genuine protection. In a Spirit of Joy Church, or any other, when joy surprises us, we think a disaster is around the corner. Transformed people are receivers of gratitude and they celebrate and can consider all things linked to the joy of the Lord. People are not aware or anticipating that joy when they are too busy chasing something extraordinary. Joy comes to us in special moments of ordinary bliss.

How can we create an environment where joy and miracles happen? Phillips Brooks would say that a congregational community must be created in which tensions from disagreements can be faced. Grace is the foundation. Regardless of the techniques used in preaching or therapeutic counseling, the bottom line is the grace of God. Brooks would agree that our vision must be to create an environment in which individuals will be accepted and the doors opened for new growth. The preacher must develop listening skills that genuinely respect the opinions of others. Harry Emerson Fosdick said, "Preaching is counseling on a group scale." A minister is concerned about the individual lives of her church members. Preaching and counseling represent two sides of a larger reality. The individual is not separated from the cultural environment. I never fully agreed with Fosdick. Effective psychotherapy takes time. Pastors and church members are not equipped to take the time necessary for life changes. There are three things a pastor can do without turning hurting people away. They can do referrals, evaluate a situation, and provide support. Serving in several differing places, pastors tend to remain somewhat personally detached from parishioners to claim the emotional freedom needed to minister to those same people in times of crisis.

These attitudes are reinforced by the professional promises that when a pastor leaves a church, she or he is required to sever relationships with the now former members. After all these years, I think it wise to make a clean break. We do release the bonds of spiritual and physical intimacy when we resign and move away. However, at least 75 per cent of most ministers' closest friends are former parishioners.

Some entering the Spirit of Anxiety Church come with racing hearts and shaking hands. They look around to see where they can sit in the pews. To quell that anxiety, they sit in the same place every Sunday. Anxious folks sit in the back or at the end of a pew. They think of making a quick escape, but they never do. An anxious woman in one of my churches drove ten times around the block before she could park and come inside the church building. She shared that singing in church caused anxiety because of thinking people are judging how she sang.

Another time of anxiety comes with the passing of the peace. This is when everyone is expected to get up and shake hands or hug to say hello. Passing of the peace can last from five to ten minutes. For the anxious, these are the longest minutes of worship. They do not like hugs or holy kisses, or handshakes and they find it painful to greet people even if they know them. When I first moved to Omaha, Nebraska, I decided to place my church membership in Westside Church. The first time I attended worship, the kind pastor said, "Now let us give a good ole Westside greeting. Would the members please stand, and shake hands, greet and hug those who are seated." My anxiety sparked. So the next Sunday, I stood up with the members so I would not be made to feel uncomfortable.

Communion is another time that anxious people get on edge and become nervous. The Christian Church (Disciples of Christ) has communion every time they meet for worship. It is difficult for some. The woman who drove around the block ten times would not partake of the communion. She said she felt unworthy. We told her that Jesus offers the Lord's Supper to all. It is especially hard to walk up to the altar in front of the whole congregation even though everyone is doing it.

"What if?" statements reveal possibilities and help in exploring anxieties and to prevent suppression. Welcome anger, fear, and anxiety. Permit the instincts, capacity to focus, and intuition flow. Dr. John Davidson related in a Psychology of Religion class at Baylor University said that his son, John Davidson, Jr., used those "what if" scenarios when doing his television shows and singing in concerts. This class stirred up my interest in studying psychology in preparation for working with people in churches where I would serve.

The only sure way out of this problem is to take a look at God's heart toward those who are anxious. Were Jesus' words about anxiety meant to be a law? No. The words of Jesus and Paul the apostle bring good news, not bad news. They offer hope and a way out, never condemnation. Take a moment and read John 14:27,

Ephesians 3:12, and II Timothy 1:7. These promises make it clear that God's desire is not to weigh us down with worry and anxiety or condemn us. The hope is that we can get better. We do not have to be miserable. Coming into real faith is the beginning of the end for anxiety.

Faith is supernatural because the Holy Spirit, working through the Word of God, creates faith in the human heart. The human mind does the believing. Faith is the opposite of unbelief or misbelief. Mistaken beliefs underline the Spirit of Anxiety Church. Faith does not mean we should quit our jobs and wait for God to provide. Jesus refused to make faith some kind of game. Read Matthew 4:5-7.

Theologian Soren Kierkegaard said, "The one therefore who has learned rightly to be anxious has learned the most important thing." This is quite close to what Aristotle said about anger. Anger and anxiety run in pairs.

The present era has been called "the age of anxiety." There have been more studies on anxiety than any other emotion. As a child, my brothers and I read *Mad Magazine*. The freckled red head looked something alike my brother David. On the cover there was Alfred E. Newman who constantly repeated, "What, me worry?" Destructive anxiety fragments life. The Spirit of Anxiety Church has an atmosphere of no peace, fretting, and complaining. Six million people in the United States are treated for General Anxiety Disorder each year.

The Spirit of Anxiety Church also must practice praying. Hopeful and joyful living are within reach. Our precious children and our older parents, job security, broken relationships, illness, destiny, and confusion stalk everyone on this life journey. Dr. John Davidson often quoted the theologian Paul Tillich, "The basic anxiety of a finite being about the threat of non-being, cannot be eliminated. It belongs to existence itself."

The church is in the business of restoring relationships with God and the children of God. We miss the mark by feeding the fire. They cannot see that they are a part of the anxiety or that they help to continue the emotional process. Becoming a Spirit of Joy congregation, the transformed folks realize that a gathered group with the joy of the Lord as their strength create the atmosphere where miracles happen, and relationships are renewed and made whole. We must be willing to cry things out, to sit with a hurting person without giving advice, and to be content just to be there for another.

Faith is a matter of action. Trusting God is acting on the basis of something we believe is so. The action that Jesus called his disciples to make denied any strategy of avoidance. To circumvent the action would have led these people to take care of their own business first, find out how to float in case of sinking first. The disciples obeyed the Lord with action. The following events cured the worry and anxiety.

Anxiety in itself is not a rejection of Jesus' call to duty and action that comes with disobedience. So we must target the avoidance behavior which means shirking the duty to which we have been called. Misbelief is one of the root problems of anxiety. We tend to avoid people, scenes, and thoughts that invoke anxious feelings. One ingredient that cannot be omitted from any therapeutic treatment is exposure to the thing that is feared. In the case of a pastor who had anxiety to the point she would not dare drive in snow. Well Nebraska had snow and ice for the whole of winter. She imagined herself driving in the snowy conditions until she stopped feeling uncomfortable. She drove out to her church office, to visit in homes and hospitals.

In chronically anxious and less mature congregations, the most reactive people are given the most attention. They are given the most say in making decisions. Anxiety raises its level throughout the group. Progress is slowed and other difficulties are quickly on the way.

In a healthy congregation, people respond, but do not react. Appreciation and discernment for each opinion is considered with openness and genuine concerns. They do resist making changes simply because the critics make demands. Healthy leaders learn from positive thoughts and are humble enough to learn.

Changes come in the wellbeing of churches. Of course, the existence of change heightens the anxiety and tension. All living things experience loss which causes grief and anxiety. Any change can bring a loss. Anxiety indicates that the person or congregation is working through the loss. There will be some resistance, so pastors or church leaders take it personally. Ministers need a non-anxious presence to prevent shutting down the process of dealing with the changes.

During the time of negotiation concerning my call to one church they said they wanted to attract youth and children. Some were quite worried about that. One enthusiastic young man professed faith in Christ. After his faith profession and baptism, he said he wanted to work with youth. He had been a drug dealer. He was enthusiastic and attracted youth like a pied piper. He was a promising athlete, participating in football and had won the state championship in wrestling. One Sunday he asked if he could preach. The older people were anxious about his speaking in the worship. His message was more of a testimony, even after I had given him some basics on preaching. There were 188 in attendance that day. The town wanted to hear about how he had changed his life. Some got jittery as he spoke. I said, "I am delighted that our youth director is preaching his first sermon this morning. I did not get a week off because he is preaching. He and I worked hard together to prepare for this special day." I keep a non-anxious presence as Tyler spoke for about an hour. After the service, a 90-year-old matriarch of the congregation remarked, "That was not my cup of tea this morning. But I love this church and we do not have to have my cup of tea every Sunday. It was such a joy to see so many young people in church."

As a psychotherapist and clergy coach, I have observed that when people become upset or angry, it is a signal that the most productive time in the treatment is imminent. Congregations must be enabled to see that anxiety is a sign of healing engagement to deal with an issue that they genuinely care about, and with God's grace, they always can work it out. Existence itself means change. The Spirit of Anxiety can trust God and together, they'll get through it. Healthy and maturing growth will become the essence of how they respond. In the Spirit of Anxiety Church, some will complain about an unrelated issue in the unconscious attempt to avoid the matter and to divert attention. If the ministers and lay leaders are tired and functioning at a lower level, some anxious members can cause trouble by lighting a fire in another place to force leaders to react instead of making a carefully thought out response. The church must be prepared for the hostility and passive aggressiveness from those who are most frustrated. Remaining calm and absorbing some of the anxiety can create immunity to the congregational body. One way to remain calm is to prayerfully remember that it is Christ's church. Christ will lead the people as they rely on the promises of God and the guidance of the Holy Spirit. Wisdom requires careful listening and learning in difficult times in order that they can serve Christ's church and help it to flourish.

A Spirit of Anxiety Church can always gain a determination to survive the challenges it faces. A commitment to persevere is a strength. That strength can become an obstacle if there are wagons tightly circled allow no change, no new leadership, and no variations of the established traditions. The anxiety from outside influence is viewed as the enemy. In the Spirit of Anxiety Church, the minister is merely tolerated in her unique ministries. The grim code often is, "We have outlived all our previous ministers, and we will outlive you also." The anxious old guard that has controlled the congregation for years no longer has the energy or interest necessary for any new programs or outreach, but they are unwilling to turn the reins over to new members. Enthusiastic young pastors who have the tools and determination and courage to revitalize the congregation brings the tension that drives pastors out of ministry.

Tradition is a powerful god in the anxious church. The demands are obeyed without question. Tradition can become a heavy burden. The church then brings on feelings of shame and guilt when committees and organizations within the church disappears. The women's group or the men's group, and youth and children's groups dwindle and die. References to the "good old days when the church was alive" reflects deep discouragement. "Our church was filled every Sunday in the 50s. We had 100 people in prayer meeting every Wednesday night. Sunday is just not sacred nowadays." The congregation must act and call for help before the level of discouragement becomes systematic and overwhelms the healing possibilities. A realistic and welcoming adjustment to old ways could have turned the tide.

One of the most amazing friends I have ever had was a man named Bill Moore. He was a member of one of my churches on the Max Meadows Circuit in Virginia. Bill looked like Babe Ruth. He had been a star on his company's baseball team. He gave me a baseball that he had hit for a home run. Bill enjoyed outdoors like I did. He served in France during World War II. One haunting war experience was when he killed his first Nazi soldier. They were behind trees. Bill shot him. Bill was sensitive and thought, "He had a family and I regretted having to kill him. I knew it was him or me."

I spent a lot of time with Bill and his grown family. His son was on home hospice. As he was dying, his son and I watched movies. We were able to laugh. The funeral was emotional and difficult for me.

Bill would often go with me to visit and to minister. We shared many times of joy on the way. Bill was a gem, a diamond in the rough. Those Blue Ridge Mountain congregations were rife with inferiority and guilt, anxiety, anger, and fear prevailed. A few like Bill were exceptions. I wanted to share my gratitude to God in this book for my friend Bill.

One story I share is about the day he took me fishing. We went to a secret pond over the mountain. We both had fishing rods. He was skillful casting his bait. When I cast mine, I hooked it into a tree limb. Bill looked at me with a big smile and said, "Now Dr. Jim, there ain't no fish up in them old trees. "With Bill's encouragement we had a most rememberable fishing day. We caught some lovely fish. Bill's wife Evelyn cooked them. What a treat to share a communion and the best fish I ever ate.

There will always be people who enjoy life like Bill Moore. The small congregation where he was a member told me that they didn't want no more members, because we do not like to pay "them asking." In those days the United Methodist Church collected apportionments or "asking." The amount was based according to the total membership reported to the annual conference.

Today their method has changed to asking every congregation to pay their mission denominational outreach with a tithe of ten per cent of the total budget. Churches have their own maturity level. Apparently when the denomination changed its system for stewardship, churches loosened their anxious grip and found new avenues for joy.

Minister surplus and the resulting tight job market causes anxiety. This new truth causes lost esteem and the perception that one's function is not important. The supply-demand mitigates against opportunities for a new place of ministry. Pastors define purposeful activity as moving on to a bigger church. The anxious pastor is not made aware that there are many more candidates than there are churches. After one pastor resigned from a 3,900-member church, there were more than 400 unsolicited names submitted with many letters from the pastors themselves within three months. Even in this reality, church leaders focus on the joy of stepping up, not stepping down. A colleague of mine with a Ph.D. from Vanderbilt Divinity School stepped down from a solid Presbyterian congregation in East Tennessee to accept a call to a rural congregation in southeast Nebraska. "Stepping down" is not always as promising.

We are living in an age of transition. We stand in a gap between the prevailing perceptions of the culture of a few decades ago in juxtaposition to the emerging images of today. It has proven that we cannot to the images of yesterday. New wine cannot be poured into old wineskins.

Anxiety causes us to be more concerned about the future in life, instead of the present reality of things. We all anxious about living in the Kingdom of God on earth today. We are plagued by anxiety. One of the representatives at a General Assembly of the Christian Church (Disciples of Christ) wore a button that read, "Jesus is coming. So look busy." Anxiety prevents us from realizing that Jesus is already among us. He is in our midst when we feed the hungry, cloth the people left out in the cold, and as we welcome the stranger.

In Luke's gospel, Jesus was asked by some anxious religious leaders when the Kingdom of God is coming. Our Lord responds that "the kingdom is not coming in things that can be observed. Some will say, 'There it is," or "There it is, over there,' but I tell you the kingdom is among you. It is already within you." Jesus is speaking of the present moment, not of what is to come in the future, but of what we already have. There is the expectation that there are many things left for us to do to create the kingdom here and now.

The prevailing anxiety about the kingdom leads some to judge who will get into the kingdom and who will be left out. The Spirit of Anxiety Church is attempting to create the kingdom by themselves. They accumulate a lot of stuff, things to give pleasure. Hording our stuff perpetuates anxiety by claiming a false sense of satisfaction with the huge amounts of worldly treasures clogging up our lives.

Our focus is on these empty treasures as we are consumed with being consumers. Releasing our anxiety about accumulating things comes if we give up getting more stuff. If we do, then we are enabled to focus on the "joy of the Lord as our strength" and enjoy the treasures of each other. A treasure that is one another is worth the energy. When we live in God's love, moments of joy happen, and the kingdom of God opens up in our midst.

Worries about tomorrow cannot define our lives today. We can live with hope and expectation as we relinquish our anxiety and begin to cherish the moments of joy here and now.

God's desire for us is to enjoy a much happier live on earth than we could imagine. We do not need to die and go to heaven to enjoy heaven. We get a glimpse of the supernatural environment of heaven. Living in heaven on earth is not inconceivable. The concept is exciting. We in Christ are already citizens of the kingdom and we have a future. In some of Jesus' parables, he spoke about the kingdom of heaven as a future reality. In other parables, Jesus indicated that the kingdom is already in progress. Matthew is where the "kingdom of heaven" is used. Mark, Luke, and John used the "kingdom of God."

In the Lord's Prayer, the Model Prayer, Jesus gives further insight into the kingdom and how it comes. Jesus taught his disciples to pray, "Your kingdom come, your will be done on earth as it is in heaven." This prayer implies that the kingdom of heaven is where and when God's will be done.

This is a prayer used in one of my weekend retreats on emotional struggles with social anxiety. "Jesus, with my upset stomach, feeling like I cannot breathe. I worry that people in this congregation will think I am stupid or annoying. I sense the urge to bolt from the group. Lord, I know I cannot see how I can do it without the

Holy Spirit. I do not expect that you simply dissolve my anxiety with no action on my part. Supply me with courage to face and endure even if the way for my freedom is difficult. I pray in the name of Jesus. Amen."

As part of the kingdom of heaven, we have dual citizenship. I have citizenship in the United States, and also God's kingdom. The kingdom came with Jesus' first coming, but there will be a future fulfillment. We are normally anxious because the Scriptures do not clearly teach that Christian believers will spend eternity in heaven when they die. Jesus did say we will live forever, but he did not say where heaven will be. He did promise eternal life. A chief message of the church is that there is a bodily resurrection from death for the people of God. We trust that God has a perfect plan. That's all we need to know.

CHAPTER FOUR

The Spirit of Guilt Church

Guilt is a universal human experience. The Spirit of Guilt congregations feed on the guilt of its members. These people continually recycle guilt. They can create it in places it did not exist previously. All have sinned. The only souls who show no guilt are psychopaths or some who are living as sociopaths. Christians devote a tremendous amount of spiritual energy dealing with sin and guilt.

Too many people beat themselves up, not because they have committed a sin, but for the temptation to commit a sin. Jesus was tempted just as we are. The reformer Martin Luther said, "You can't keep a bird from landing on your head, but you can keep it from making a nest in your hair."

Some people feel a false guilt if they have not heard from God. We sense God when we pray or when we read the Word of God. Loving God is not evidenced by outward things like dancing in the spirit or squishy feelings of euphoria. We can measure our emotions moment to moment as we demonstrate our live for God by our actions.

Some have a false guilt about not being sanctified. Sanctification does not complete itself in just a moment. It is a slow process that takes a lifetime. We continue to learn that we are always loved. Our sinful tendencies will not be completely overcome. My brother Edward does the iron man and marathons. He knows he cannot just run and run, but in his preparation, he trains to run each day. Running further and further every day, he runs further in time in the Boston Marathon, the Iron Man events in Hawaii, Quantico, New York, he has accomplished all of these.

Actual conviction over actual sins is not the same as false guilt over false expectations. Doubt, temptations or the absence of "correct" emotions and the slow pace of sanctification masquerade as reasons to feel like a failure. Christ will complete the good work that the Spirit of Joy started as a grace-motivated effort. Refuse to be defeated by things the Bible never says we must do.

Guilt spreaders cite that one wrong is equal to one bad person. They are approval addicts. They never can get enough. One nice word will not sustain them. Self-esteem is sucked out of others. They cannot receive and enjoy good gifts because they never feel they deserve any affirmation or gifts. Being compulsive comparison addicts, they just hate it when another congregation is happy. They are also obsessive moralizers. An act or thought is either right or wrong, black or white, or good or bad. They feel immoral when they do most anything that should bring delight. They have a difficult time grasping God's grace.

Spiritual abusers tap into this spiritual drive that all people live with and manipulating it for their own purposes. Awareness of personal guilt resides deep in our souls. There is no struggle more difficult than overcoming a sinful habit.

Guilt does not motivate people to change. Revivals in every generation and Christian eras spread throughout the world enhanced by guilt-producing sermons. Those raised during the Great Depression respond to guilt sermons, but the new generations will have no part of it. They turn deaf ears to them.

Guilt arises when our boundary has been broken from inside by some action, we have done wrong or something people convinced us was wrong. Dealing with our guilt can bring integrity, self-respect, and atonement by behavioral changes. Guilt is a valuable emotion for awareness of our thoughts, our physical desires, our spiritual longings, our being haunted by improper behaviors, addictions, and compulsions. Our ethics become compassionate. We can judge and supervise our own behavior.

We feel shame as a consequence of guilt and wrongdoing. If we cannot say, "I am ashamed of myself, we will never improve. Shame is a master teacher for emotional channeling. Shame can strengthen us, but it puts us out of commission immediately. If we welcome shame, we won't do something inappropriate and we'll get firmly out of the way of temptation. Authentic shame will stand in your inner boundary and observe everything going on out of our soul. We gain self-respect that leads to higher happiness and contentment. Bearing shame will keep us from being victimized by those in the Spirit of Guilt churches with their schemes.

We live in a world where we think shames is good. Some use shame to keep people in line. How tragic it is when shame leads to violence, aggression, bullying, eating disorders, and addictions. A sense of shame can help us keep boundaries. Shame reminds us of our limitations.

Shame in a scarcity culture cause us to not feel good enough. We are trapped within social boundaries. Our focus is to enable ourselves to improve. Focusing only on ourselves ends with discouragement. If a minister's vision and motive for being a pastor is "meeting people's needs," are dangerous to themselves and to a congregation that lacks a clear sense of who they are as they constantly feed their own egos. Effective ministers are grasped by something bigger than themselves. Morality comes as a by-product of the attachment of being claimed, owned, prepared for larger purposes. Guilt and shame are often buried so people get easily angered, suspicious, jealous, and arrogant. They force their vision on others in subtle ways. Sadly, they are unteachable. Those who disagree struggle and are eventually emotionally destroyed. They are competitive and afraid they could be pushed aside and lose their power and authority. Shame-based fear keeps them out of being just ordinary. Underneath the image portrayed is an emptiness filled with envy. At the core of this emptiness lies internalized shame.

Few of us have faced our authentic shame and remorse. We were taught about shame by being shamed. Authority figures attempt to control us by applying shame from the outside instead of trusting our ability to moderate our behaviors. Without connection to our own shame, powerful people will try to control and disgrace us. This coerces people into embodying others' ideas of what's right or wrong. We are then overwhelmed by foreign messages, inauthentic shame, lies, and damaging contracts. Most of us have no skills to deal with shame. We feel disgraced and spiral down in esteem that is not necessary. We feel strong and aware. Authentic shame stops our impulses, our seductive intensities, brings working boundaries. Otherwise, we act like young children in full-scale rebellion, breaking the rules, blurt out ugly words out, and turn red after the damage is done.

We will then not have tools for restoring wholeness. Behavior control will be forced on us. If we can welcome shame, we can get the strength to amend our ill-conceived behaviors and to throw off the guilt-trippers that disrupt your authenticity with incredible energy.

Guilt-trippers use a scorning mocking look, or harsh words, or silence. The apostle Paul suffered a thorn in the flesh, some unknown infirmity. The Galatian church welcomed Paul. In Galatians 4:14, he wrote, "Though my condition was a trial to you, you did not scorn or despise me, but received me as an angel of God, as Christ Jesus."

During our older years, our time becomes more acute. We can make sufferings an obsession. In spite of fatigue, we like Paul, want to continue our life journeys and calling. At each age, living is choosing. If I were to give up preaching just because retired pastors are "put out to pasture," envy and jealousy and feelings of shame because traditionally Wesley never quit until he died at 88 years old. Billy Graham lived and served somewhat even at age 100. I continue my writing ministry, as Paul did, or else I would feel guilt and shame. I also feel guilty about being in such good health when my sisters and brothers in ministry suffering sickness. I enjoy being a pastor, therapist, writer, and coach when so many people feel negative emotions with the burden of doing a job they despise. The majority feel ashamed in their obscurity, anguish, and unhappy lives. We need to be faithful despite our limitations which results in a clear conscience.

The spiritual life or ministry does not alleviate shame and guilt. The nearer we get to God, the more we experience of grace. Grace does not exempt people from sins in ourselves, and we continue unforeseeable and transient guilt.

Psychology and healthy ministers speak about true guilt and false guilt. Guilt feelings can be aroused by the suggestions of the Spirit of Guilt Church or society as a whole. Their condemnation has zeal, energy for convincing others that their views are the only views in line with God's definitions of what is evil or prohibited. Guilt results from asserting boldly or also from being silent. The fear of being judged is intensive. Local churches and denominations fear each other as they accuse each other of not being faithful. No conflict is as horrid as those born in secret.

Congregations can suppress guilt or liberate from guilt. Some remove the guilt, others increase guilt. Every minister and therapist have encountered people who believe they have committed the unpardonable sin. They read and hear sermons and teachings based on Mark 3:29, "Whoever blasphemes against the Holy

Spirit never has forgiveness but is guilty of an eternal sin." I believe Jesus is addressing the self-righteous who hold no conviction of guilt. That one refuses salvation and the gift of the Holy Spirit. When this situation is discussed, I tell those feeling this deep guilt that if they are worried about it means they have not committed any unpardonable sin. The grace of God does not remove guilt, but grace removes condemnation. "There is therefore no condemnation," Paul assures us.

Authentic guilt and shame contribute to the focus on soul-searching. Emotions are not for punishing us, but to heal us. Shame strengthens our inner boundary and restores our integrity. In the Spirit of Guilt churches, the spiritual abusers accuse members of false motives, improper attitudes, and a favorite the sins of omission which are lethal as most of us cannot defend ourselves, and by these thoughts to manipulate us and the people around us who hear the accusation as well. We experience an emotional roller-coaster controlled by the leaders' approval or disapproval of us.

I wrote *The Silence of the Church: The Spiritual Struggle with Sexuality* in 2017 with the goal of teaching churches to deal with God's gift that has been abused in so many ways in today's world.

Nothing brings on more guilt and shame than sexuality, the most uncomfortable subject. Creating an atmosphere for joy and miracles will help more people to discuss matters of sexuality. In the Spirit of Guilt Church there is no appreciation for sexuality as God designed it. They offer nothing to protect sexual integrity, sexual awareness, and sexual fulfillment.

All types of churches need to define sexuality as something that is integral to our beings. A young woman who serves as a pastor wisely said, "It is difficult to separate sexual energy from an energetic sense of aliveness in general." Sexuality is an unavoidable topic. Acceptance of healthy views of sexuality brings wholeness. Sexual energy is not just a personal energy but interpersonal energy. The positive role that energy plays in a congregation will be directly proportional to every person being able to exercise self-control. We need boundaries and accountability to help us. No pastor wants to fall into temptation. Church leaders judge other people by their works. Pastors judge themselves for their intentions. The congregation needs ethical, theological, and biblical framework for guidance on healthy sexuality. God did not create our sex drives to bind us into shame. We grow up with dangerous notions or just plain ignorance about sex. We place sex and shame in the same box. The perspective must change from merely avoiding sex and any conversations about it because of shame to acknowledging it as sacred and beautiful, something to respect.

My book highlights the fact that churches neglect to talk about sex. The truth can heal the Spirit of Guilt Church and set her free. Holding shame and guilt leads to deception and isolation. When the congregation hears the word "sex," all they can think about is "sin." They believe that we cannot have sex, even within a marital relationship except with the intension to reproduce. Sex is not a gift to be enjoyed. We are all human beings. When we try to see what's right or wrong according to culture. In determining what is wrong, we attempt to avoid temptation in our own strength. Those who do will fall and be trapped in shame.

Guilt deepens into shame as accusation, doubt, ignorance and humiliation replaces God's original design. People of all ages are confused by their sense of pleasure and curiosity. They remain silent as they surmise that our appetite in our bodies will result in ultimate destruction.

We cannot run from the fact that couples in ministry have sexual difficulties. In the average congregation, at least a third experiences sexual struggles with a cloud of corruption, abuse, confusion, and disappointment. We refuse to deal with sexuality even though the imaginations, thoughts, and sex preoccupation fill our lives. Pastors leading the Spirit of Guilt congregation has the cultural idea that sexuality is a source of discomfort. Pastors who preach and write and counsel people find that even to acknowledge sexuality arouses suspicion and criticism.

Pastors of strong integrity express that integrity in the quality of normal relationships. In a healthy community, a network of relationships is enjoyed with various degrees of closeness and intimacy. They realize and understand their vulnerabilities to sexual compromise, guarding sexual health integrity by observing boundaries that protect them from deterioration.

A healthy understanding and practice of sexuality is a large part in the mosaic A human body learns how to respond to sexual cues signaling an opportunity for sexual arousal. The cues are highly individualized and there are both male and female patterns of response. There is a problem when we experience sexual arousal and response before we are educated to understand what has happened to our bodies.

Do we not realize that in current culture children and youth are encouraged to experiment with adult sexual behaviors? Even kids in elementary school form strong associations in the early formative years of development experience disappointment and confusion when these young ones become adults and try to maintain and establish healthy sexual intimacy. Human response does not know the difference between a context of moral compromise and the opportunity for sexual pleasure. This brings confusion even when we are in a context where we are free to exercise sexuality without guilt or shame.

Healthy emotional adjustment and identity formation requires healthy sexual identity and functioning. Church leaders embrace the life journey of discovering sexuality including the apostle Paul who did not hesitate to address sexual issues with the ones in the churches for whom he felt the responsibility to instruct and encourage. We must have courage to confront sexual sin and corruption. We must balance our words with sensitivity and compassion for one of God's children caught in the traps of sexual compromise. Sexual temptation, preoccupation to the point of addiction, and enticements are everywhere. And yet the Spirit of Guilt congregation remains ignorant about the most basic information. Most presume they already know all about sexual interest, arousal, and functioning. Thousands are trying to heal and recover from sexual trauma. Their entire being recalls the sight, sound, smell, and sensation of improper touch and multitudes of wounds of sexual trauma.

When Paul writes in Galatians 5:19, he begins communicating about our sinful nature with sexual immorality. God's gift of sexuality is a most potent capacity to express the image of God in us. When this gift is corrupted, we find evil separation from that spiritual spirit that we need. This corruption is a deep source of shame.

Some dangerous signs in any congregation includes sexual innuendo in conversations, intuition of not feeling right, a member of the opposite sex wanting too much time and attention, sharing some intimacies not called for, sexual fantasy, and sexual gestures and body language. Responsibility leads a church leader to set limits and to never take advantage of any situation. She or he must be alert and aware of what might not be as innocent as it looks.

The Spirit of Guilt Church has many addicts. Drug and alcohol dependence results from genetic inheritance or experience. The unique taste and preference for mood changes, pain, or the search for love without dejection or injury. Addicts keep secrets to ensure that nobody challenges her judgment about the indulgence. Millions are now addicted to prescription drugs. There has never been such a drug problem in all of history. Drug abuse leads to sex trafficking, divorce, loss of jobs, and compromise of sexual integrity. Compromise shows. Others recognize the grip of deception long before a guilty person becomes aware of the slide to moral failure. A sweet irresistible perfume is sensed along with sexually arousing clothing and a woman might casually say, "The better to seduce you with my dear." The fantasy begins as she later says, "Nobody could love you like I can." He thinks and dreams often enough that the transition to pursuing the relationship is smooth and imperceptible as the vulnerable man is caught up in the drama of imagination, lust, and desire.

When anybody is longing to find some affirmation and validation, being intimate is emotionally intoxicating. To be healed from shame, we need to come to terms with the emotions about those who have shamed us. We must have the courage to preach forgiveness. Some leaders think that they are not allowed any affirmation. A woman came up to a male pastor telling him how tremendous his sermon was one Sunday. He responded that it all Jesus and that he could not take the credit. Her response was, "Well, it really was not that good."

The congregation harboring guilt and shame, lacking grace and forgiveness, extreme authoritarian, rigid, black and white rules and doctrine, shall ultimately become disoriented when life does not meet their expected outcomes.

The sexual safety of an entire congregation comes with focus of sexuality and integrity in classes, retreats, conferences, and continuing education. In Romans 8:5, Paul writes, "Those who live according to the sinful nature have their minds on what that nature desires; but those who live in accordance with the Spirit have set their minds on what the Spirit desires." Our confidence depends on the joy of the Lord as our ultimate strength. We need the courage to address the many issues of life including harmful addictions.

Shame and pride contain opposite emotions. Shame is feeling unworthy and unacceptable resulting in loss of pride. As shame is healed, pride is restored. The solution is to discern between healthy and unhealthy pride. The definition of pride that we must run away from is called arrogance.

People are condemned to shame by bad memories. None of us can escape from the reality that she once harmed another person. For healthy healing one must go back and review those memories and bring into the light of grace. People who can never get out of shadows in the cycle of shame dwell in the shadows of family, or parents. Guilt is like a mafia of the mind. Some even feel condemned by their own dreams. The problem comes when there is no separation from those dreams. Toxic shame is seen as spiritual bankruptcy.

We tell God we are guilty and that we need forgiveness. In any Christian congregation, we declare that "if we confess our sins, God will forgive our sins and cleanse us from all unrighteousness." (I John 1:9) We are all guilty sinners, but some people just cannot handle guilt even if they have confessed and asked for forgiveness. The experience may have been in the past, or the person they sinned against may now be deceased. They just cannot bring it to a close. The damage is irreversible. And we can never create a new past. We might even keep the pain alive for other people including friends and family. We could write a letter of apology in our journal. We have the need to finish things. Perhaps it would take a restitution.

A woman who drove around the block 12 times before coming inside felt too wicked to be forgiven. They think somebody who did the things they did should not receive forgiveness. They think they should get punishment. They do not understand that Jesus received the punishment. They have a distorted belief that they need to do good deeds to off-set the bad deeds. After having an affair, some get into a spiritual snare. Wallowing in guilt, they stay in the prison of guilt and shame. Past regrets cause the present and the future to be miserable. The sin is forgiven, but the consequences remain. Destructive guilt is past oriented. If the Spirit of Guilt Church has turmoil and pain, forgiveness brings peace and joy.

Guilt is a most subtle negative pattern. Guilt causes separation. It does not possess grace. When we feel guilty, we mess up our lives as we do not feel worthy of success. Guilt becomes a protection plan we sell to ourselves to avoid anticipated punishment. We think, "If only I suffer enough, God will forgive me." Some guilty people have the illusion that pain brings redemption.

Back in 1962, I served as summer missionary with the Home Mission Board of the Southern Baptist Convention in New Mexico. One day, I was led to a strange place that had blood stained into some rocks. It was a ritual site of the Penitentes. They are a religious sect. They practice self-flagellation, and even crucifixion. These death sites are highly secret.

No matter what extremes we use to punish ourselves, guilt is never satisfied, so we can gloat in our suffering. Guilt is a separation insurance. We must forgive ourselves for attracting punishment to ease the pain of our guilt. Toxic church groups and religious sects teach us that we are sinners. Some resent hearing this. This teaching tells us that God has condemned us. We then begin a spiritual quest, searching for the right preacher, guru, teacher, or therapist.

Matthew Fox tells us that we can think in terms of original innocence, not original sin. We think we live in paradise permanently lost. We confuse guilt and conscience. We listen carefully to the voice of guilt. Guilt is our mind disapproving of ourselves. Conscience reminds our minds of what we value. Some call it a "guilty conscience." Conscience is not guilt. The Spirit of Wisdom drives our guilt up and out. That is how we restore our innocence.

We cannot heal a whole congregation of guilt and shame. We can help restore individuals in that group. Some helpful healing thoughts are I forgive myself for thinking I was separate. I forgive myself completely. I have compassion without taking on others' pain. I am declared innocent.

Freedom from guilt and shame comes with acceptance of God's grace. God is honored when his children do their best to make things right with God, ourselves, and others. And then we are free to move forward in a positive and graceful way. With that we will no longer feel guilty as together we become a Spirit of Joy Church.

CHAPTER FIVE

The Spirit of Joy Church

The Spirit of Joy Church is filled with energy, sensuality, optimism, positivity, surprise, hope, and wonder. I have interviewed thousands asking about their times of joy. In journals, I write down the joy videos in my own life journey. Later as I have to deal with guilt, fear, anger, anxiety, and guilt, I remind myself of "the joy of the Lord" and those joys experienced by others. Joy shared is joy multiplied. People smile as they share their joy. And they feel honored as they feel warmth inside and out. Joy is a time we are breathless. The memory of blissful moments is never forgotten. I have shared psychology of joy as a college and seminary professor, as a writer publishing more than 40 books on joy, as a preacher of thousands of sermons based on joy, as a clinical therapist leading people to heal from their negative emotions and to tap into natural joy, and as a researcher on joy for more than 50 years, including a dissertation written at the University of Oxford on "Integration of Joy in Clinical Family Counseling." As a pastoral visionary, my vision "to create an atmosphere where joy and miracles happen" has influenced everything I have done in ministry.

In a sermon on the passionate joy as fire delivered at the Mennonite Health Assembly held in South Carolina, I compared joy to fire. I said, "Like fire, I gain energy from what I experience and totally consume it. Like fire, I generate heat and light. Like fire, I expand freely in all directions. Like fire, I dance in the air. Like fire, I ascend to the heavens. Like fire, I burn with hunger for more life. Like fire, I am deeply involved in my experience. Like fire, I leave nothing behind me. Like fire, I am filled with creative passion. Like fire, I consume all obstacles and use them for fuel. Like fire, I inspire people with my intensity. Like fire I warm people with my passionate joy." Mennonites are a great resource for mental health and emotional issues. During the world wars, Mennonites served passionately in mental health hospitals because they are conscientious objectors. That service perhaps directed them to do such excellent work in removing the stigma and silence on mental health concerns.

Joy is an emotion that comes through all five senses. Joy is in a loving touch or sexual pleasure. Tasting a fresh peach or peach ice cream or any fruit brings a time of joy, smelling roses in a garden, hearing inspiring music, and the sight of a loved one or a new baby brings delight.

Feelings of joy are contagious in congregations. A Spirit of Joy Church celebrates joyfulness and lets it flow naturally. Joy cannot be conjured up or created by oneself. Joy will seek you out at a surprising time in connection with others. Joy is the one emotion we believe will continue in our anticipation of heaven and we will have made peace with our fears, anger, anxiety, and guilt.

Joy is said to be an orgasmic emotion as a peak experience. Joy offers relief from the bonds of our life journey. It frees us from the difficulty of dealing with other feelings as it appears spontaneously to give you wonderful sensations all parts of us are awakening to be touched by this rare and radiant bliss.

Joy shows up after we have come a long way to the end of a journey. Our joy comes as we finish the years of academic study and receive our reward, a degree that we see as significant and vital for success. Joy brings an ultimate and mysterious gift from heaven or the cosmos as magic. Joy ebbs and flows in response to our work and our contentment. Even in a Spirit of Joy communion, we live in a real world where we must feel all our honest emotions, and joy will inexorably find us. These communities endure honest hardships, ordeals, loss, love, laughter, and grief.

If one has no idea how the emotion joy intersects with our lives, we can be seduced into communion with people whose lies include that we can be joyful all the time. Unfortunately, when life's difficulties arise and the falsely exhilarated leaders in the high control communions clash with reality, a mess is created. We need to focus and ground ourselves, or we might fall for the scammers of false joy. The uproar is a natural reaction to emotional imbalance. This occurs when any of our feelings are imprisoned. Remember that no emotion is bad or good. All emotions are natural and necessary reactions. Find a more centering on joy anticipation and realize that we have more work to do and more life to live.

When we find ourselves in any manipulating fire-only practices, we must protect ourselves and our friends and family for their own health. Churches with exhilaration addiction and cultic ways are sharing an endangering state that requires more help than most people can provide.

Write a new ending for yourself, for those we serve and support. Honestly, I feel anxiety and nervousness when I teach or preach. People in the pews offer me their most precious possession, their time. Ministers are vulnerable and the words, our images, and stories pull us apart or bring us together.

No person or group can selectively numb emotions. If so, we numb the light and the dark shadows. Should we numb our pain, our grief by default we take the edge off our joy experiences. Getting stuck in that place is not helpful. Theologian Rob Bell observed, "Despair is the belief that tomorrow will be just the same as today." This despairing stance is devastating. Daring spiritual leaders are never silent about the hard times in their lives. The Spirit of Joy communion share a way of believing that involves the values that are most important. It professes values, but more important they join together to practice them.

Besides joy, the Spirit of Joy Church holds sacred values such as loyalty, freedom, family, faith, justice, usefulness, serenity, love, success, wholeheartedness, wisdom, vision, travel, courage, excellence, uniqueness, intuition, and cooperation.

The atmosphere with these positive values stands on the side of the poor. This attitude makes the stand to serve difficult people. Life is not faced in a casual way as others suffer. No one is allowed to suffer from the lack of meeting basic human needs because of a lack of awareness. This community feels God in the eyes of the poor, those without merit in in life's daily journey. They train disciples to be aware of those living on the street, in hard corners of the town, in situations most ignore. They are happy people calling on their goodness, values for others. The sacred values elicit well-being and hope, laughter, and newness. These are signs of folks filled the spirit of the joy of the Lord sharing lavishly as love is spread around to all who need it.

Love motivates the children of God to do something new and to work with imagination and creativity to see miracles happen. The church's ministry happens on the way to something else. Miracles come unexpectedly with strangers and when they are aggressive in demanding unjust things to stop. Joy snowballs in connection with others. Like Jesus, they will to interrupt their journeys, their lives to bring abundant life for others. What mercy they do for the rejected, the helpless, the poor, the ostracized is interpreted as doing these acts for the person of Christ.

They are themselves not unaware of human suffering. They feel helpless as they face evil. As children of God of any age, they are utterly sincere, loving for the sake of loving. Love sleeps and waits in little people's lives. The Bible says that we are children of God. Even if our childhood was not good, we still have one with God. They proclaim the stories of God about being children in the kingdom. All are called to sustain, create, and make life, especially the lives of the weak and needy other children. From their day of birth, young children learn from adults. The children, the least of us reach out to God. Some churches stand in God's way offering more anxiety, fear, anger, and guilt.

Historically, the church has been designed for adults. Jesus told us we must become children.

The task for the Spirit of Joy Church is difficult. Children watch and criticize and become just like the adults who refuse to grow up. Most church members want to be taken care of rather than do the will of God. We are the children of God. We are to be God's servants. We are the body of Christ and we are to be God's hands to touch others. We are God's feet to go forth to engage the poor. God uses our bodies, our words, our arms to care for the children.

When I studied at Baylor, I traveled with the Baylor Evangelistic Association conducting revivals and youth crusades in Texas churches. We made a mission trip to Juarez, Mexico. Juarez is a border town across the Rio Grande from El Paso, Texas. One preacher in our group pointed out, "There are first world nations, second world countries, and third world countries. And then there are the Mexican border towns." The poverty was beyond anything I had ever seen. Thousands live in cardboard boxes covered by corrugated tin roofs. Dust hangs around in a cloud that lingers on. The revival tent meeting gave us close contact with the suffering children and adults. We came to know that any attractive woman could not find a job anywhere. With no other choices available, they entered the ugly field of prostitution. People would offer their daughters, as young as age 12, for sexual favors for a price. Their stories of life across the border were beyond imagination. The conditions were more horrid then any places I have visited to share Christ in poor nations. My stomach turns in knots as I think about it.

The most endearing memory of that first trip to any foreign nation was the joy of worship in the churches that invited us. One congregation was named Verdad Y Luz, or in English, the Truth and Light Church. People were faithful to worship in a crude building as if their lives depended on it. There was no judgment there. The joy shown on their faces was overpowering and contagious. Where in the world I thought would families join and embrace the joy of the Lord in a place where babies are starved, and life is so limited. Yet there they were showing more joy than any of us had experience across the border in affluent United States. Joy surprises us when God is present, where there is little but sincere hope that things will get better. Joy can happen in a small cinder block church. When C.S. Lewis was teaching at the University of Oxford he gave his autobiography the title, *Surprised by Joy*.

Lewis was probably the first Christian writer to say that joy surprises. Joy comes an experience unplanned and unbidden. Joy cannot be coerced into reality. It has its own timetable. The Spirit of Joy blows where it wills.

Lewis tells of his first experience with joy that he could remember. He was about five years old. Lewis recognized joy when his brother Warnie made a little toy garden of flowers and twigs in the lid of a biscuit tin. The enchanted Lewis thought of its beauty. He longed for that kind of beauty the way he thought about heaven. Joy for Lewis was a desire to be with God. He wrote that we are like an ignorant little child who goes on making pies in a slum area, because she cannot imagine what is meant by the offer of a vacation at the sea shore.

Joy is a gift, not a reward. The French philosopher Blaise Pascal said, "Nobody has more joy than a professed Christian." Sometimes I attempt to dream that one of the young women who professed faith in Christ at our Juarez revival created her own atmosphere and the impossible happened. She might have gone through the ordeals to become a citizen of the United States, went to college and seminary and is now a missionary to the people of Mexico.

In the Westminster Confession of Faith, the question is asked, "What is the chief end of humankind?" The answer: Our chief end is to glorify God and enjoy (God) forever."

A healthy Christian church shares and practices the message that Christ taught us about loving one another and God. In a healthy congregation, members are as much a part of the ministry as the spiritual leader. Unhealthy churches reject, stigmatize, misunderstand, and victimize, but a healthy community becomes a refuge for those in need. These needy families are in quest for restorative relationships and a healing environment that encourages loving relationships. This atmosphere provides a safe spiritual atmosphere for everyone including the pastors.

They are aware of their own mission. They handle negative emotions. They welcome new members. They respect one another's boundaries. They insist on open communication. And they anticipate the joy of the Lord for the future. They experience growth as individuals as well as the church. To be a healing congregation, it must be noted that the "joy of the Lord is our strength." Members will see that each person is made in God's image worthy of grace and respect.

Fredrich Schilling's *Ode to Joy* is a powerful musical piece that is a thread for living with life to the fullest.

"Joy is called the strong motivation in eternal nature.

Joy, joy moves the wheels in the universal time machine.

Flower it calls forth from their buds, suns from the Firmament.

Spheres it moves far out in Space where our telescopes cannot reach.

Joyful, as His suns are flying across the Firmament's splendid design.

Run brothers, run your race, joyful as a hero going to conquest."

The Spirit of Joy Church realizes that life is more than something to be endured. Life is more than survival. Life is not easy. We must live in a place where all emotions are felt. The happiness of life with all its pain can be recovered with our innocence. Feeling releases the numbness from our bodies. We are free to dream, to renew our faith, to be romantic, and to awaken ourselves to new excitement and precious moments of pure joy.

Healthy congregations are comfortable with differentiation, a sense of autonomy, and aware of their vulnerability. The pastor does not accept unrest personally. As anxiety appears, few are contaminated by it and are enabled to help individuals cope or problem solve as a connected body of Christ.

Robert Louis Stevenson expressed it well, "To miss the joy is to miss everything." Joy is the missing ingredient in the contemporary church. Joy is a forgotten tribute of God. Joy is a road sign pointing us to God. The inner joy of Jesus came from the Father. Kenneth Wolfe, my Hebrew professor at Midwestern Baptist Theological Seminary in Kansas City, had us write down and describe an attribute of God. I wrote my paper on joy. I found more than 100 Hebrew words for joy. My quest brought me to Isaiah, Nehemiah, Zephaniah, and even in Ecclesiastes, I rejoiced in the joy of the Lord as my strength.

The reason God has led me to research and write so many books on joy is to experience how joy can be appropriated in the congregations. We sense emotions of joy in new converts as they believe and are baptized into faith. Our lives glow with fruitful abundance. Throughout scripture we are told the message of salvation in Christ is joy. The first fruit of the Spirit is love. The second fruit is joy. Joy surprises us as we don't have to be religious with God. Joy is not something we do. It is a gift of the Holy Spirit. Grace comes from God with no effort from us. Joy is wrapped up within the gift of grace. Joy is the badge of the person who is in touch with the living God. The church has been crippled in her walk with God because of a lack of the spiritual fruit of joy.

The Spirit of Joy Church gives us a fresh experience of authentic joy. Take the "joy of the Lord" into church. We can be touched by a new burst of ebullient joy. We need to communicate in our teaching, preaching, writing, and counseling that those who know Jesus the Christ will be the most joy-filled people in the world.

The Prayer of Saint Francis describes the Spirit of Joy Church. "Lord, make me an instrument of your peace. Where there is hatred, let me sow love. Where there is injury, pardon. Where there is doubt, faith. Where there is despair, hope. Where there is darkness, light. And where there is sadness, joy. OH divine master, grant that I may Not so much seek to be consoled as to console, to be understood as to understand, to be loved as to love. For it is in giving that we receive. It is in pardoning that we are pardoned, and it is in dying that we are born to eternal life. Amen."

PRACTICAL APPLICATIONS

Chapter One - Spirit of Fear Church

Where have you experienced ecclesiophobia? Describe your experiences of fear in congregations.

Chapter Two - Spirit of Anger Church

How does anger affect the leaders?

How does it cause job insecurity?

What must be protected? What must be restored?

Chapter Three - Spirit of Anxiety Church

How does anxiety keep us miserable?

What does non-anxious presence mean?

Chapter Four - Spirit of Guilt Church

What is guilt and false guilt?

How do power groups use guilt?

Chapter Five - Spirit of Joy Church

How do we focus on joy?

Describe joy in a congregation.

How can focus on joy be dangerous?

AFTERWORD

Dr. John Killinger

Jim McReynolds and I have spent more than a lifetime in joyful friendship.

Almost every time I hear from him, he is engaged in some new and happy adventure.

There are few nations and territories he has not touched. The idea and movement of Spirit of Joy churches is unique and wonderful. This has never been more needed than today, when many traditional churches are floundering because of poor leadership and simple faith fatigue.

Jim has served as Minister of Joy to the World in his calling as an apostle of joy. His healing and vulnerability and courage are demonstrated in his writing, teaching, counseling, and preaching for more than half a century.

His idea of Spirit of Joy churches is a Johnny Appleseed kind of thing that just might spread like wildfire throughout the world that is hungering for authentic love and faith.

Dr. John Killinger

BIBLIOGRAPHY

Benyei, Candace. *Understanding Clergy Misconduct in Religious Systems.* New York: Haworth Press, 2001.

Blanchard, Ken. *We Are the Beloved.* Grand Rapids: Zondervan, 1996.

Bilich, Marion, Susan Bonfiglio and Steven Carlson. *Shared Grace: Therapists and Clergy Working Together.* New York: Haworth Press, 2000.

Bry, A. *How to Get Angry Without Feeling Guilty.* New York: New American Library, 1990.

Bonhoeffer, Dietrich. *Life Together.* San Francisco: Harper Collins, 1954.

Bronson, Po. *What Should I Do with My Life?* New York: Random House, 2002

Buechner, Frederick. *Telling Secrets.* San Francisco: Harper Collins, 1991.

Buford, Bob. *Finishing Well.* Brentwood, Tennessee: Integrity Media, 2006.

Fortune, Marie. *Sexual Violence: The Sin Revisited.* Cleveland: Pilgrim Press, 1999.

Friedman, Edwin. *Generation to Generation.* New York: Guilford Press, 1985.

Goleman, Daniel. *Emotional Intelligence.* New York: Bantam Books, 2004.

Greenleaf, Robert. *Servant Leadership.* New York: Paulist Press, 1990.

Henderson, Hazel. *Building a Win-Win World.* San Francisco: Berritt-Koehler, 1998.

Lev, Rachael. *Shine the Light: Sexual Abuse and Healing in the Jewish Community.* Boston: Northeastern University Press, 2002.

Lew, Mike. Victims No Longer: *The Classic Guide for Men Recovering from Child Sexual Abuse.* New York: HarperCollins, 2004

Long, E.L. *Patterns of Church Polity: Varieties of Church Governance.* Cleveland: Pilgrim Press, 2002.

Melton, Joy. *Safe Sanctuaries: Reducing the Risk of Child Abuse in the Church.* Nashville: Discipleship Resources, 1998.

McClintok, Karen. *Preventing Sexual Abuse in Congregations.* Herdon, Virginia: Alban Institute, 2007.

McClure, John and Nancy Ramsey. *Telling the Truth: Preaching About Sexual and Domestic Violence.* Cleveland: United Church Press, 1998.

O'Grady, Ron. *The Hidden Shame of the Church.* Geneva: World Council of Churches, 2001.

Ormerod, Neil and Thea. *When Ministers Sin: Sexual Abuse in the Churches:* Alexandria, Australia: Millennium Books, 1999.

Papeo, Daniel. *Bowen Family System Theory*. Boston: Allyn and Bacon, 1990.

Riley, Reba. *Post-Traumatic Church Syndrome*. Indianapolis: Chalice Press, 2015.

Rilke, Rainer Maria. *Letters to a Young Poet*. New York: Vintage Books, 1996.

Tillich, Paul. *The Courage to Be*. New Haven: Yale University Press, 1952

Williamson, Marianne. *The Healing of America*. New York: Simon & Schuster, 2000.

Zarra, Ernest. *It Should Never Happen Here*. Grand Rapids: Baker Books, 1997.

I do hope you have enjoyed

THE SPIRIT OF JOY CHURCH

It has been an awesome privilege to write for you.

May God bless you with a spirit of joy.

Dr. James McReynolds, D.Div., Th.D., Psy.D., Ph.D.

ABOUT THE AUTHOR

The Spirit of Joy Church has been birthed following a lifetime of serving the church. Dr. James McReynolds has been a servant of those seeking how to deal with human emotions as a therapist, a preacher, a teacher, and as a writer.

During a School of Practical Christianity in New York, Norman Vincent Peale anointed him in the oil of joy as the Minister of Joy to the World.

Jim first pursued joy in a Hebrew course at Midwestern Baptist Seminary in Kansas City. He wrote a paper on the Hebrew words for joy in the Old Testament. Dr. John Killinger, his major professor for the master and doctoral programs at Vanderbilt University Divinity School, has been a close friend who has called him the "Apostle of Joy."

Born in Kingsport, Tennessee, he had a humble beginning. His family lived in a small one-room apartment. His delivery was done by a physician who had attended Carson-Newman College and the University of Tennessee. Little "Jimmy" was born on a Tuesday. The following Sunday, he was enrolled in the cradle roll at the First Baptist Church in Kingsport. Jim was the first person in his family to ever attend college.

His life has been filled by incredible and surprising experiences. The joy of the Lord has been his strength given through grace.

Index

1950's bulletins, 30

A
Abingdon, 5
abuse, 20, 35, 52, 67, 75, 117
  angry, 76
  drug, 120
  sexual, 24, 35, 146
  spiritual, 35
  substance, 22
abuse power, 75
Abusers, 19
abusers, male, 35
abusive spouses, 61
accountability, 116
accumulating, 105
accusation, 115, 117
accusations, false, 57
accuser, false, 57
act crabby, 23
activity, 24, 47, 103
  human, 60
actualizing, 18
Adam, 61
addictions, 15, 50, 110–11, 119, 122
  exhilaration, 129
addicts, 64, 120
  approval, 109
  compulsive comparison, 109
  religious, 19

adults, 21, 35, 61–62, 119, 131–32
affirmation, 29, 74, 109, 121
AFTERWORD, 7, 144
age, 14, 17, 32, 95, 104, 113, 117, 131, 133
  middle, 63
  wiser, 55
aggression, 22, 111
agoraphobia, 43
air, 72, 127
  fresh, 67
Alban Institute, 146
alcohol centers, 15
Alexandria, 146
Alfred, 95
aliveness, 15, 116
Allyn, 147
Amazonia, 5
ambiguities, 75
ambiguous thoughts, 52
amen, 76, 107, 138
American families, 25
Anabaptists, 48
anger, 9–10, 13–14, 20, 22–25, 38, 41–43, 49–54, 56–69, 72, 77–82, 95, 102, 126, 128, 131
  anger begets, 50
  channel, 56
  directed, 22
  emotion, 22–23, 53
  expressed, 83
  expressing, 80
  healthy, 14, 56, 59
  quick to, 51

repress, 22
repressed, 57
resolved, 59
understanding, 23
unhealthy, 22
unresolved, 58
welcome, 94
Anger Church, 7, 50, 56–58, 61, 65, 67, 70, 140
Anger Churchdom, 23
anger congregations, 72
anger energy, 65
anger-free life, 77
anger management, 59, 76
anger management courses, 77
anger management therapy groups, 52
angry abusers blame, 61
angry atmosphere, 50, 62, 82
angry blowups, 63
angry experience, 22
angry explosions, 62
angry minister, 58
angry profane words, 67
anguish, 57, 77, 114
   emotional, 89
annual conference, 103
anonymous essay, 25
anonymous rhyme, 54
anticipation, 83, 128
anxiety, 9–11, 13, 20, 42, 68, 70–71, 76, 83–90, 93–100, 102–7, 126, 128–29, 131, 136, 141

basic, 96
Anxiety Church, 7, 20, 83, 85, 87, 93, 95–96, 99–100, 105, 141
anxiety churches, 70
anxiety clashes, 84
anxiety gnaws, 85
anxiety reducer, 86
anxious attention fade, 86
anxious feelings, 97
Anxious folks, 93
anxious members, 100
anxious paths, 90
apathy, 14, 55, 57
apostle, 39, 94, 144
apostle of joy, 149
apostle Paul, 113, 119
APPLICATIONS, 7, 139
appointments, 49, 72
apportionments, collected, 103
apprehension, 88
Aristotle, 52, 95
arousal, 119
   sexual, 118
arousing clothing, 121
arrangement, 33
arrogance, 122
ASB Bridge, 33
Ashland City, 5
athletes, best, 30
atmosphere, 17, 20, 28, 30, 38, 63, 70–72, 96, 116, 126, 130, 134–35
attachments, 69, 111

form, 57
attendance, 34–35, 99
Australia, 146
Authentic guilt and shame, 115
authenticity, 32, 65, 113
   crave, 77
Authentic shame stops, 112
authoritarian, 19
   extreme, 121
authorities, 41, 75, 112
authority figures, 112
avarice, 23, 25, 59–61
Avaricious, 25
avenues, new, 103
avoidance behavior, 97
awakening, 128
   spiritual, 19
Awareness of personal guilt, 110

B
Babe Ruth, 101
babies, 26, 133
   new, 127
Bachelor, 33
Bacon, 147
Baker Books, 147
balance, 119
   finding, 47
   restore, 90
Bantam Books, 145
baptism, 98
   believer's, 48
   infant, 48
Baptists, 48

Baylor, 132
Baylor Evangelistic Association, 132
Baylor University, 94
beat, 108
   job environment, 59
behaviors, 18, 63, 110, 112
   adult sexual, 118
   anti-social, 22
   exterior, 16
   ill-conceived, 113
   improper, 110
beliefs, 14, 95, 130
   distorted, 123
believers, 26, 32, 69
believing, 95, 130
Beloved, 145
Benyei, 145
berated Moses, 80
bereavement, 25
Berritt-Koehler, 146
bias facts clog, 31
Bible, 32, 47, 63, 78, 89, 109, 131
biblical evidence, 81
biblical framework, 116
BIBLIOGRAPHY, 145
Bilich, 145
Bill, 101–2
Bill's encouragement, 102
Bill shot, 102
Bill's wife Evelyn, 102
birth order, 57
biscuit tin, 134
bitterness, 57–58, 80

Black Preaching, 29
black religious experience, 29
blame march, 61
Blanchard, 145
blessings, 41, 68, 77
blinding mist, 72
bliss, ordinary, 91
block, 50, 75, 93–94, 123
Blue Ridge Mountain congregations, 102
Blue Ridge Mountains, 34
boards, 31, 33, 45
Bob, 145
bodies, 10, 16, 24–26, 33, 40, 85, 90, 117–18, 132, 136
  connected, 136
body language, 16, 52, 120
body sensations, 21
body tenses, 52
bonds, 92, 128
Bonfiglio, Susan, 145
Bonhoeffer, 145
book highlights, 117
border, 133
border town, 132
Boston, 48, 146–47
Bostonians, 48
Boston Marathon, 109
boundaries, 10, 14, 56–57, 67, 110–12, 116, 135
  anger sets, 55
  healthy, 57
  inner, 111, 115
  new, 67
  observing, 118
  social, 111
  well-defined, 41
boundary setter, 59
Bowen Family System Theory, 147
boys, 35
boys experience crushes, 35
brains use, 46
Brentwood, 145
Brick Church, 34
Brick United Methodist Church, 5
Bristol, 5, 25
Bronson, 145
Brooks, 48–49, 91
brother David, 95
brother Edward, 109
brothers, 22, 26, 68, 95, 113, 136
brothers Jim, 11
brother Warnie, 134
Brushing, 38
brush strokes, 11, 39
Bry, 145
buckle seat belts, 40
budget, total, 103
Buechner, 145
Buford, 145
bulging eyes, 69
burn, 59, 127
burst, new, 138
business, 96–97
business partner, 19

C
Camden Point, 5
Cameron, 5, 36
Candace, 145
capacity, 56, 94
  potent, 120
cardboard boxes, 132
care, 24, 47, 67, 74, 79, 86–87, 97, 99, 132
Carlson, Steven, 145
carpet, new, 31
Carson-Newman College, 149
cast, 61, 86, 102
casting, skillful, 102
celebrate, 65, 91
celebration, 20
celebrities, 23, 60, 66
CEOs, 66
Chalice Press, 147
change, 17–19, 38, 41–42, 49–50, 61–62, 65, 69, 73, 98–100, 110, 116
change heightens, 98
change pastors, 75
change perception, 70
Chapter Five, 143
charismatic, 67
cheeks wee flaming, 54
cheerleaders, popular, 30
child, 10, 57, 63, 95
  estranged, 26
  grown-up, 63
  ignorant little, 134
Child Abuse, 146
childhood, 35, 63, 76, 131

Childlike faith, 63
child relearns, 62
children, 10, 17, 30, 32, 34–35, 37, 42–43, 61–63, 87, 98, 119, 125, 131–32
  precious, 96
  suffering, 132
  target, 35
  women abuse, 35
  young, 112, 131
children copy, 63
children of God, 96, 131–32
children's groups dwindle, 101
children's guilt, 63
Child Sexual Abuse, 146
Christ, 5, 46, 58, 65–66, 82, 94, 98, 100, 104, 106, 109, 131, 134–38
  body of, 90, 132
Christ atrophies, 33
Christian believers, 107
Christian Church, 65, 94, 104
Christian congregation, 123
Christian eras, 110
Christian Ethics, 33
Christian faith, 17
Christian history, 68
Christianity, 43, 65
Christian love, 30
Christians, 24, 27, 41, 43, 108
Christians and congregations fear, 83

Christian servant, 72
Christian tradition, 23
Christ Jesus, 9, 73, 113
Christmas Carol, 18
Christ Memorial Baptist Church, 5
Christ's church, 100
Chronic anger, 50
church administration, 33
church body, 74
church building, 43, 93
church call, new, 67
church community, 18
church culture, 24
church dynamics, 39
churches, 13, 15–21, 24–36, 38–40, 42–45, 48–50, 57–60, 63–68, 70–72, 74–76, 92–94, 98–101, 103, 115–17, 146
  3,900-member, 103
  anxious, 101
  average, 34
  conservative, 42
  contemporary, 137
  early, 69
  healthy, 11, 77
  institutional, 74
  local, 31, 114
  perfect, 13, 39
  purest, 39
  teaching, 115
  toxic, 28–29, 31
  traditional, 144
  welcoming, 30
churches change, 19
churches circuit charge, 34
churches lock, 40
churches use, 42
church families echo, 62
church family, 71
church fellowship, 84
church fights, 31
Church Governance, 146
church history, 33
  modern, 33
church leaders, 52, 64, 74, 76, 91, 98, 119–20
church leaders expound, 79
church leaders focus, 103
church leaders judge, 116
church members, 58, 60, 92, 132
church membership, 93
church office, 97
Church Polity, 146
church record, 48
church services, 83
church shares, 20, 84
  healthy Christian, 135
cinder block church, 133
citizens, 106, 134
citizenship, 107
  dual, 107
claim, 73, 92
classes, 29, 94, 122
Classic Guide, 146
clean break, 92
clergy, 23, 37–38, 49
  coach, 38

clergy coach, 42, 99
clergy gathering, 76
clergy killers, 42–43
clergy persons experience, 66
clergy turnover, high, 37
Clergy Working, 145
Cleveland, 145–46
clients, 14, 53–54, 68, 83, 88–89
  phobic, 44
Clinical Family Counseling, 126
Clinical therapists, 35, 126
cloud, 117, 132
coach, 77, 113
coaching ministry, 44
coach potato, 60
code, 64
  grim, 100
Coercion, 58
college, 11, 45, 126, 134, 149
college campus, 84
colored lenses, 73
colors, 13, 31, 72
Colossians, 69
comfort, 49, 65, 83
comfortable position, 51
Committed Christians, 32
communion, 33, 94, 102, 128
community, 17, 34, 57, 67, 70–71, 76, 128, 130
  caring, 32

congregational, 91
  healthy, 118, 135
community gathering, 32
community groups, 57
community service, 27
community shifts, 17
companion, 29
  constant, 40
companions, close, 25
company's baseball team, 101
compassion, 19, 65, 119, 125
Compassionate prayer, 70
competition, 31, 42
complain, 68, 99
complaining, 20, 96
complicating worries, 90
compromise, 120
  moral, 119
  sexual, 118–19
compulsions, 15, 110
computer screen, 85
conceptions, 74
condemnation, 69, 94, 114–15
condescending, 22
Cone, 29
Cone, James, 29
conferences, 122
confession, 78, 80
conflict, 31, 37, 52, 59, 114
  stirring, 38
conflict mediator, 59
confrontation, 26

Confronted, 52
confusion, 70, 72, 79, 87, 117, 119
confusion stalk, 96
congregational body, 100
congregational contenders, 48
congregation harboring guilt, 121
congregations, 17, 27–28, 31, 33–37, 58–59, 64–65, 67, 73–78, 98–101, 103, 109, 111, 114, 116–17, 120
  affluent, 37
  average, 117
  dominated, 42
  dream, 13, 16
  fearful, 42
  imperfect, 39
  local, 42
  mature, 97
  nourishing, 17
  rural, 104
  single, 39
  solid Presbyterian, 104
  strict fundamentalist, 68
congregations fear, 83
congregations teach, 80
congregation's theology, 20
Connecticut, 13
connection, 67, 78, 112, 128, 131
Conquering anxiety, 86
conquest, 58, 136

conscience, 125
  clear, 114
conscience reminds, 125
conscientious objectors, 127
constraints, 68
  financial, 37
consumers, 31, 105
contact, close, 132
content, 7, 77, 96
contentment, 111, 128
context, 119
contracts, 112
  unhealthy, 59
control, 29, 50, 63, 75, 85, 112
  behavior, 113
  lost, 61
control communions clash, high, 129
conversations, 29, 116, 120
  painful, 66
conviction, 109, 115
Corinth church, 71
Corinthians, 71
corners, hard, 130
corporate attorney, 63
corrugated tin roofs, 132
corruption, 117, 119–20
couch potato, 25
Council Bluffs, 5
counseling, 44, 92, 138, 144
  pastoral, 33
  required angel management, 53

therapeutic, 91
counseling clients, 38
couples, 25–26, 117
courage, 65, 77, 82, 87, 101, 107, 119, 121–22, 130, 144, 147
covetousness, 23
cradle roll, 149
creativity, 66, 87, 131
crises, worst, 45
crisis, 38, 89, 92
  spiritual, 38
crowds, large, 48
crucifixion, 124
cues, 118
  emotional, 14
cultic ways, 129
cultural boat, 41–42
cultural idea, 118
culture, 14, 16–17, 30–31, 104, 117
  healthy, 30
  toxic, 30
culture children, 118
cup, 99
cycle, 88, 122
Cy Young, 29

D
Daddy, 43
damage, 56–58, 112, 123
  soulful, 56
dangers, 14, 40
  constant, 68
  physical, 90
  real, 40
Daniel, 145, 147

Daniel Boone Baptist Chapel, 5
Daring, 130
darkness, 65, 85, 138
daughters, 36, 43, 133
  middle age, 64
  young, 63
Davidson, John, 94, 96
days, 24–25, 29, 36, 39, 49–50, 74, 81, 99, 101–3, 109, 124, 131
  fishing, 102
  hard, 27
days Winter Convocation, 72
D.Div, 148
deacons, 26, 31
deaf ears, 110
death, 48, 61, 70, 86, 107
death sites, 124
deception, 117, 120
deeds, 123
  bad, 123
defeatist thoughts, 89
degrees, 68, 118, 128
  right, 52
Delaware, 45
delight, 24, 110, 127
demographics, 30
denial, 24, 77
denominations, 17, 28, 32, 35, 37, 43, 59, 103
  state Anglican, 48
denominations fear, 114
depensation, special, 33
depression, 14, 22, 43, 55, 60, 68

crippling, 86
persistent, 68
depths, 28, 32, 75
Desensitization, 90
design, 117, 136
despair, 27, 29, 87, 130, 138
desperate, 16, 28
destiny, 32, 96
Destructive anxiety fragments life, 95
Destructive guilt, 123
deterioration, 118
devastation, 42
Dickens, 19
Dickens, Charles, 18
Dietrich, 145
differentiation, 136
digestion, incomplete, 65
digestive issues, 44
disagreements, 91
disappointment, 28, 66, 89, 117
development experience, 119
disapproval, 115
disapproving, 43
discernment, 98
disciples, 39, 97, 106
 train, 130
Discipleship Resources, 146
Disciples of Christ, 65, 94, 104
discouragement, 72, 101, 111
disillusionment, 29

disillusions, 50
disobedience, 97
dispositions, 20, 28
dissertation, 126
distances, 36, 39, 76
 safe, 87
divert attention, 99
Divinity degree, 33
divorce, 42, 57, 120
doctor, 44, 85
doctoral programs, 149
doors, 20, 25, 40, 92
dread, 70, 88
dreams, 13, 121–22, 134, 136
 ole, 73
driver's seat, 41
drug, 15, 120
drug dealer, 98
DSM IV label, 88
Dust hangs, 132
duty, 97
dysfunctional abuses, 35
dysfunctions, 16

E
earth, 104, 106
earthly ministry, 80
Easter, 40
East Side Baptist Church, 5
East Tennessee, 104
eating disorders, 111
eating shelter, 60
Ecclesiastes, 137
ecclesiophobia, 42–44, 139

ecumenical activities, 40
edge, 94, 129
Edwin, 145
Effective ministers, 65, 111
Effective psychotherapy, 92
effort, 62, 73, 137
　grace-motivated, 109
egocentric anxieties, 71
Egypt, 80
El Paso, 132
embarrassment, 83
embroidered clothing, 21
emotional benefits, 89
emotional channeling, 111
emotional imbalance, 129
emotional intelligence, 21, 145
emotional issues, 127
emotional pain, 87
　chronic, 51
emotional reactions, 62
emotional roller-coaster, 115
emotional thrust, 45
emotion joy, 16
emotion joy intersects, 128
emotions, 10, 13–18, 20–21, 28–29, 37–38, 51, 53, 59, 77–79, 86, 88, 108, 110, 114–15, 127–29
　correct, 109
　crippling, 85
　harmless, 56
　honest, 128
　human, 14, 149
　intelligent, 10, 40
　label, 14
　life's, 79
　negative, 38, 126, 135
　numb, 129
　opposite, 122
　orgasmic, 128
　repress, 15
　repressing, 15
　self-defining, 56
　sense, 137
　squelch, 14
　survival, 53
　understanding, 20
emotions flow, 15
empathic minister, 13
Emphatic skills, 13
emptiness, 112
encouragement, 79, 85, 89
　permanent affirming, 73
energy, 41, 53, 56, 65, 72, 85, 100, 105, 114, 116, 126–27
　healthy, 90
　interpersonal, 116
　personal, 116
　sexual, 116
　spiritual, 108
enmeshment, 55–56
entertainment, 31
enticements, 119
entitlement, 37

environment, 28, 48, 56, 59, 63, 65, 70, 84, 91–92
　cultural, 92
　hurtful, 29
　right, 75
　supernatural, 106
　toxic, 19
Ephesians, 47, 58, 95
Ernest, 147
Escalation, 52
escape, 16, 88, 93, 122
Evansville, 5
Eve, 61
evil, 58, 61, 114, 131
　human, 43
evil separation, 120
examination, 51
excessive anxiety, 51
excitement, new, 136
exodus, 19, 79
expectations, 26–28, 67, 105
　false, 109
　unrealistic, 69
Expecting, 50
experience, 18, 20, 37, 43–44, 50, 55, 62, 66, 114–15, 118, 120, 123, 127, 133, 137
　common, 64
　first, 134
　fresh, 138
　peak, 128
experience anxiety, 87
experience avoidance, 43
experience growth, 135
experience loss, 98

experience panic attack cycles, 41
Explosive anger, 62
extraverts pull, 84
an eye for an eye, 52

F
faces, 17, 100, 133
facial expressions, 16, 52
failures, 58, 109
　moral, 121
　personal perceptions, 73
faith, 26, 28–29, 39, 41, 49, 51, 66, 68, 70, 72, 86–87, 95, 97, 134, 136–38
　professed, 98, 134
　real, 95
faith community, 70
faith fatigue, 144
faith profession, 98
families, 25–26, 35–37, 42, 50, 53, 57, 61–62, 79, 81, 88, 90, 102, 122–23, 129–30, 149
　angry, 62
　indulgent, 62
　needy, 135
　untraditional, 34
family members, 42
family services, 15
fans, 23, 60
fantasy, 121
　sexual, 120
faring, 23, 60
father, 21–22, 63, 80, 137

father's joyful reception, 21
fault finder, 22
fear, 9–10, 13–14, 23, 25, 40–47, 57–58, 64, 66, 68, 70, 76, 78–80, 83, 87–88, 126
    fear Church lets, 41
    healthy, 44
    identifying, 46
    intense, 84
    irrational, 42
    pastor's, 45
Fear Church, 7, 20, 40–41, 44, 47, 56, 139
fear churches, 43
Fear congregations, 10, 41, 44, 47
fear dreads, 41
fear-filled atmospheres, 86
Fearful Church, 40
fear paralyzes, 25
fear retreats, 40
fears condition, 83
fear zone, 47
feeding, 58, 96
Feeling Guilty, 145
feeling unworthy, 122
fellow practitioner, 73
fellowship, 26, 71, 73
    welcoming, 27
female patterns, 118
female teachers, 35
Finishing, 145
Firmament, 136

First Baptist Church, 48, 149
first Baptist congregation, 48
First Christian Church in Weeping Water, 78
First Presbyterian Church, 5
First United Methodist Church, 5
fish, 33, 102
    best, 102
    lovely, 102
fishing rods, 102
flame, 61
    candle, 51
floundering, 144
Flourishing congregations, 17
flowers, 134, 136
fog, 73
    heavy winter, 72
folks, 60, 130
    transformed, 96
football, 62, 98
foreign nation, 133
forgive, 123–25
forgiveness, 69, 81, 115, 121, 123
forgive ourselves, 124
formative years, early, 118
Fortune, 145
Fosdick, 92
Fox, Matthew, 124
France, 101
Francisco, San, 145–46

freckled red head, 95
Frederick, 145
Fredrich Schilling's Ode, 135
freedom, 107, 125, 130
  anxiety constricts, 87
  emotional, 92
French philosopher Blaise Pascal, 134
fresh peach, 127
Friedman, 145
friend Bill, 102
fruit, 73, 127, 137
  first, 137
  forbidden, 61
  spiritual, 11, 137
frustrated volunteers, 37
Fuck, 60
fuel, 38, 51, 127
fulfillment, 107
  sexual, 116
fundamentalist, 42
fury, 14, 67
  raging, 24
fuse, short, 51

G
Galatian church, 113
Galatians, 113, 120
game, 29, 95
gap, 37, 104
garden, 127
  little toy, 134
Gate City, 5
gatekeepers, 20, 45
General Anxiety Disorder, 96
General Assembly, 104
generalizations, 58
Generalized Anxiety Disorder, 88
generation, 18, 25, 53, 110, 145
generational, 38
generations, new, 110
genetic inheritance, 120
Geneva, 146
genie, 71
genie power, 71
Gentiles, 66
gentleness, 69, 71
gestures, 52
  aggressive, 69
  sexual, 120
Gethsemane, 70
get rid, 69
ghosts, 19
giant sculptures, 48
gifted students, 30
gifts, 13, 39, 70, 73, 79, 109, 115, 117, 120, 134, 137
  mysterious, 128
  special, 33
girls, 25, 35
  teenage, 26
glazed eyes, 53
Glenwood, 5
gluttony, 23–24, 59–60
goal, 69, 72, 85, 115
  spiritual, 69, 81
  unattainable, 51
God, 26–29, 47–49, 67–75, 77–81, 83, 86–87, 91,

94–96, 99–100, 104–8, 113–17, 119–20, 123–25, 130–35, 137
  glorify, 134
  living, 137
  praise, 68
  protest, 78
  reason, 10, 137
  sense, 108
  time grasping, 110
  trust, 80, 99
God bless, 148
God cares, 87
God choices, 79
God experience anxiety, 43
God-given feelings, 15
God help, 60
God to get rid of anger, 69
golden calf, 80
golden rule, 31
Goleman, 145
Good News, 32
goods, worldly, 69
gossip, 76
  unhealthy, 31
grace, 7, 13, 26–27, 36, 39, 47–48, 77, 81–82, 91, 110, 114–15, 121–22, 124–25, 135, 137
Graham, Billy, 113
Grand Rapids, 145, 147
gratitude, 66, 69, 91, 102
Great Depression, 110
Greatness, 66
Grecians, 39

Greek, 33
greener pastures, 37
Greenleaf, 146
grief, 79, 98, 128–29
grip, 120
  anxious, 103
ground ourselves, 129
group, 26, 29, 40, 43, 56, 58, 65, 84, 87, 97, 101, 106, 125, 129, 132
  angry, 67
  gathered, 96
  healthy, 40
  support, 66, 73
  women's, 101
group cluster, 84
group scale, 92
growth, 27
  maturing, 99
  new, 92
  nurture character, 32
grumbling Israelites, 79
guidance, 32, 100, 116
guides, 19, 69
Guilford Press, 145
guilt, 13, 20, 42, 50, 57, 64, 68, 101–2, 108, 110, 112–17, 119, 122–26, 128, 131
  confuse, 125
  false, 108–9, 114, 142
  suppress, 114
  transient, 114
guilt and shame, 112–13, 116, 123, 125

Guilt Church, 7, 20, 108, 114, 116–17, 120, 123, 142
guilt churches, 111, 115
Guilt congregation, 108, 118–19
guilt deepens, 117
guilt feelings, 114
guilt sermons, 110
guilt spreaders, 109
guilt-trippers, 113
guilt-trippers use, 113
guilty, 113, 115, 123–25
guilty conscience, 125
guilty sinners, 123

H
habit, 84
  sinful, 110
Hallsville, 5
happiness, 15, 89, 111, 136
  highest, 17
hardest seasons, 73
hardships, 77
  honest, 128
Harming ourselves, 81
Harper Collins, 145
HarperCollins, 146
Harry Emerson Fosdick, 92
hate, 24, 58, 64, 84, 109
haunting war experience, 102
Hawaii, 109
Haworth Press, 145
Hazel, 146

heal, 41, 90, 115, 117, 119, 125–26
healing, 14, 17, 19, 38, 72, 77, 90, 144, 146
  healthy, 122
healing congregation, 135
healing emotion, 11
healing engagement, 99
healing environment, 135
healing flow, 41
healing memories, 78
Healing of America, 147
Healing of memories, 77
Healing of souls, 18
healing thoughts, 56, 125
health, 20, 113, 129
  long-term, 65
  mental, 127
  spiritual, 46
health problems, 51
  mental, 77
Healthy congregations, 98, 135–36
Healthy emotional adjustment and identity formation, 119
Healthy leaders, 98
healthy ministers, 114
heart rate, 44
  racing, 69
hearts, 10, 26–27, 62, 65, 81, 94
  broken, 26
  human, 95
  racing, 93

heaven, 39, 106–7, 127–28, 134
  kingdom of, 106–7
Hebrew Bible, 33, 79
Hebrews, 39, 137, 149
  academic teaching, 33
Hebrew words, 9, 137, 149
help individuals, 136
helpless, 61, 131
helplessness, 51
help track, 90
Henderson, 146
Herdon, 146
Hidden Shame, 146
historic Boston churches, 48
history, 120
  denominational, 33
Holy, 114
holy ground, 26
holy kisses, 93
Holy Spirit, 71, 78, 95, 100, 107, 115, 137
home, 27, 48, 62–63, 83, 88, 97, 101
  pastor's, 74
  returning, 25
  spiritual, 13
  unhealthy angry, 61
  wealthy, 30
home hospice, 102
Home Mission Board, 124
honesty, 65
  raw, 72
Hopeful, 96
hopelessness, 79–80
  expressing, 79
Hording, 105
horrid, 114, 133
hugs, 93
Human action, 52
human beings, 117
human body, 118
human emotion, normal, 53
human existence, 29
human experience, universal, 108
human feelings, 21
human proportions, 23
human response, 20, 119
humans, 20, 27–28, 60, 68, 75
  gathered, 87
human system, 59
humiliation, 117
humility, 65, 69, 71, 75, 86
hunger, 64, 127
hurt, 9, 38, 42, 45, 50, 53, 57, 64, 66, 69, 76–77, 83, 88
hurt Job, 79
husbands, 47
hymns, 30, 36
  spiritual, 36

I
ice, 53, 97
identity formation, 119
idolization, 71
i feel, 16

ignorance, 117
  plain, 116
Ignorance and silence on sex, 35
II Corinthians, 46, 77
II Timothy, 95
Ill health, 88
illness, 9, 96
  mental, 42, 89
  psychiatric, 15
  terminal, 9
illusion, 91, 124
illusory self-perceptions, 69
images, 21, 50, 71, 104, 112, 120, 129, 135
  emerging, 104
imagination, 118, 121, 131, 133
imperfections, 19, 65
improper attitudes, 115
improper touch, 119
impulses, 50, 112
  uncontrollable, 61
incompetence, 67
incongruent, 52
inconveniences, 83
incredible energy, 59, 113
Indiana Pilgrim Presbyterian Church, 5
Indianapolis, 147
indignation, 57
individuals, 50, 92, 125, 135
Ineffective behavior, 52
inferiority, 45, 102

infirmity, unknown, 113
inflaming situation, 38
inflammation, 21
information storage, 2
ingredient, 97
  missing, 137
injury, 120, 138
injustices, 17, 27, 61
innocence, 124–25, 136
insensitivity, 51, 56
insufferable restraints, 68
Integration, 126
integrity, 50, 110, 115, 118, 122
  sexual, 116, 120
  sexual health, 118
Integrity Media, 145
intellect, 66, 90
Intense activity acts, 47
intensity, 83, 127
intentions, 15, 116
interpersonal relationship issues, 51
interventions, 21, 38
  miraculous divine, 49
intimacies, 37, 118, 120
  healthy sexual, 119
  physical, 92
Intimidation, 58
intoxicating, 121
introverts, extreme, 84
intuition, 120, 130
  unlimited, 90
intuition flow, 94
invitation, 26
invulnerability, 91

Iowa Calvary Baptist Church, 5
Iowa Hillcrest Baptist Church, 5
iron, 109
irresistible perfume, 121
irritations, 51, 67, 89
Isaiah, 137
isolation, 55, 117
　complete, 20

J
James, 62, 86
jealousy, 56, 64, 113
Jesus, 10–11, 17, 27–28, 66, 68, 70, 80–81, 86, 94–95, 97, 104–8, 121, 123, 131–32, 137–38
Jesus' call, 97
Jesus is coming, 104
Jesus' joy, 75
Jesus' parables, 106
Jesus sweat blood, 83
Jesus' words, 94
Jewish Community, 146
Jim, 9–11, 102, 144, 149
Jim finding, 9
Jimmy, 149
Jim's oil paintings, 11
Jim states, 10
job insecurity, 140
job market, 103
job security, 41, 96
John, 94, 106, 123, 146
John Killinger BIBLIOGRAPHY, 7

Johnny Appleseed kind, 144
Johnson City, 5
journal, 51, 81, 123, 126
Journaling, 46, 69
journeys, 89, 128, 131
　daily, 130
　earthly, 70
　restless, 39
joy, 9–11, 13–15, 17, 20–21, 70, 72–73, 78–82, 87–89, 91, 102–6, 126–28, 130, 133–38, 143–44, 148–49
　authentic, 138
　ebullient, 138
　false, 129
　inner, 137
　recognized, 134
joy anticipation, 129
Joy Church, 1–150
joy churches, 36, 144, 148
joy communion, 128
joy communion share, 130
joy congregation, 96
joy ebbs, 128
joyful, 21, 96, 128, 136
joyful atmosphere, 59
joyful friendship, 144
joy of the Lord, 75, 138
the joy of the Lord, 36, 59, 126
joy of the Lord as our strength, 105

joy of the Lord is our strength, 135
joy snowballs, 131
joy surprises, 91, 133, 137
joy videos, 126
Juarez, 132
Juarez revival, 134
judgment, 25, 68–69, 120, 133
just get over it, 84
justice, 48, 57, 68–69, 130
juxtaposition, 104

K
Kansas City, 33, 36, 137, 149
Karen, 146
Keene, Priscilla, 25
Ken, 145
kids, 30, 118
Killinger, John, 13, 144, 149
Kill or be killed, 53
kindness, 69, 81
kingdom, 32, 104–7, 131
kingdom of God, 32, 63, 73, 86–87, 104–6
Kingdom of God on earth, 104
kingdom peace, 75
kingdom person, 62
Kingsport, 149
Kingston, 5
Kingsville, 5
knowledge, 10, 21, 74, 81

intuitive, 81
Knoxville, 5

L
language, 60
laughter, 128, 130
law, 94
  dysfunctional, 68
lawyers, 68
  angriest, 68
leaders, 16, 33–34, 37, 58, 65, 91, 99, 115, 121, 140
  anxious religious, 104
  elected, 76
  exhilarated, 129
  force, 100
  ministerial, 45
  spiritual, 58, 130, 135
  young, 26
leadership, 17, 20, 34
  conference, 74
  denominational, 41
  new, 100
  pastoral, 17
  poor, 144
leadership positions, 19
lean, 69, 72
lessons, 26, 78
letters, 71, 103, 123, 147
  scarlet, 26
Lev, 146
levels, lower, 100
Lew, 146
Lewis, 133–34
life, 9, 14–15, 17–18, 49–50, 64, 66, 70–71, 79,

85–89, 103–4, 121–22,
129–31, 133, 135–36,
145
life energy, 84
Life in spiritual
gatherings, 70
life journeys, 89, 96, 113,
119, 126, 128
lifesavers, 10, 40
life's difficulties, 129
lifetime, 48, 109, 144,
149
life vision, 14
Light Church, 133
lightheartedness, 23
limitations, 45, 111, 114
Lincoln, 36, 60
listening skills, 92
little messes, 11, 39
London congregation, 70
lonesome valley, 73
longs, 26
Lord, 9, 70, 73, 79, 81,
86–87, 91, 96–97, 104,
106, 122, 130, 133, 135,
137–38
Lord's Prayer, 106
Lord's Supper, 94
Losing my control, 53
loss, 75, 83, 87–88, 98,
120, 122, 128
  boundary, 55
lost it, 61
a lot of joy, 36
Louisville Medical
School, 71

love, 25–27, 32, 34, 36,
51, 53, 56, 64, 66–69,
71–72, 74–75, 81–82,
120–21, 130–31, 137–38
  authentic, 144
  eternal, 26
  given, 34
  little, 66
  neighbor, 71
  sow, 138
  unconditional, 48
love God, 71
love ourselves, 67
loving, 13, 15, 17, 71,
131, 135
Loving God, 108
loving relationships, 135
loving touch, 127
Luke, 106
Luke's gospel, 104
lust, 23–24, 59–60, 121
lust and gluttony, 24, 59–
60
Luz, 133

M
Mad Magazine, 95
magic bullet, 20
manipulation, learned, 63
manipulation help, 58
Manipulations, 63
Marianne, 147
Marie, 145
Marion, 145
Marley, Jacob, 19
marriage counseling
sessions, 61

marriages, 57, 62
master, 110, 149
   divine, 138
Matthew, 86, 95, 106
maturity level, 103
Max Meadows Circuit, 101
McClintok, 146
McClure, 146
McReynolds
   brother Edward W., 45
   David H., 9, 11
   James, 1–2, 148–49
   James C., 21
   Jim, 144
McReynolds INTRODUCTION, David H., 7
mechanistic procedures, 47
medication, 44
meeting
   outdoor, 84
   revival tent, 132
meeting people, 111
Melton, 146
members, 27–28, 31, 45, 47, 62, 64, 74, 81, 83, 88, 90, 92–93, 101, 103, 135
   new, 101, 135
members gang, 31
membership, 74
   total, 103
membership rift, 19
members squabble, 19
memories, 18, 57, 77, 122, 126

bad, 122
endearing, 133
Mennonite Health Assembly, 127
Mennonites, 127
mental abilities, 57
mental health hospitals, 127
mental health issues, 76
mental health practitioner, 15
   licensed, 14
mental health stigma, 84
mercy, 56, 131
mess, 73, 124, 129
messy, 9, 76
Methodist elder, 33
Metropolitan Tabernacle, 48
Mexican border towns, 132
Mexico, 132, 134
middle ground, healthy, 15
midst, 48, 87, 104–5
Midwestern Baptist Seminary, 149
Midwestern Baptist Theological Seminary, 137
mighty challenges, 9
Mike, 146
Millennium Books, 146
mind disapproving, 125
minds, 28, 31, 35, 38, 50, 77, 88, 122, 125
   human, 95

ministering, 69, 75
ministers, 13, 16, 44, 47, 49, 58, 60, 64, 66, 74–76, 87, 92, 98–100, 102, 144
ministers fear, 15
Ministers Sin, 146
minister surplus, 103
ministry, 16, 35–37, 44–45, 48–49, 65, 73, 75–76, 78, 101, 103, 113–14, 117, 126, 135
  church's, 131
  unique, 100
ministry sucks, 72
miracles, 17, 70, 78, 91, 96, 116, 126, 131
misbehavior, 58
misbeliefs, 89, 95, 97
misconception, 35, 78
misguided interpretation, 70
missionary, 134
  summer, 124
Missouri, 5, 36
Missouri Amazonia United Methodist Church, 5
Missouri Camden Point Baptist Church, 5
Missouri First Christian Church, 5
Missouri Immanuel Lutheran Church, 5
Missouri Kingston Christian Church, 5
Missouri Kingsville Christian Church, 5

Missouri Saint John's United Church of Christ, 5
misunderstand, 135
misunderstood, 84
mocking, 89
  scorning, 113
Model Prayer, 106
Moffitt, Phil, 18
mom, single, 26
moments, 46, 48, 66, 105–6
  blissful, 126
  precious, 136
  special, 91
money, 61, 85
Moore, Bill, 101, 103
Morality, 111
moral structure, 56
motivation, 51, 66, 85
  strong, 135
motives, false, 115
mountain, 73, 102
movement, 144
  calming, 90
movies, watched, 102
multitudes, 79, 119
music, 22
  hearing inspiring, 127
  soft, 51
music lessons, 62

N
Nashville, 5, 146
nations, 144
  first world, 132
  poor, 133

natural flow, 56
natural joy, 126
natural reaction, 129
Nazi soldier, first, 102
Nebraska, 5, 36, 42, 60, 93, 97
  southeast, 104
Nebraska Shenandoah Presbyterian Church, 5
negative actions, 18
negative events, 18, 68
Negative feelings, 28
negative grin, 11
negative pattern, 124
negative self-images, 37
negative sentiments, 79
negative thoughts, 46
negativity, 20, 58
negotiation, 98
Nehemiah, 137
Neil, 146
nervousness, 88, 129
nervousness overwhelms, 83
New American Library, 145
newest book, 9
Newman, 95
New Mexico, 124
Newport, 48
New Testament, 27, 86
New Testament congregations, 33
New wine, 104
New York, 109, 145–47, 149
Nicomachean Ethics, 52

nightmares, 16, 30
non-Christian, 13
non-experienced experiences encode, 18
Norman Vincent Peale, 10, 29, 149
Northeastern University Press, 146
numbness, 136
  emotional, 15
numbness spills, 15
nursery volunteer, 26

O
Oates, Wayne, 71
obedience, 47, 75, 86
obsessive moralizers, 109
offenders, 77
offends, 53, 80
offenses, 23–24
office, 85
  therapist's, 63
O'Grady, 146
oil paintings, 39
Older adults, 63
older brother, 9, 21–22
  healthy, 22
older brother grumbles, lost, 22
older years, 113
Old Testament, 60, 149
ole Westside greeting, 93
Omaha, 5, 36, 72, 93
one-room apartment, 149
oppression, 17, 42
ordained Jim, 10

ordained minister, 14
ordeals, 128, 134
organizations, 101
Ormerod, 146
ostracizing, 47
outdoors, enjoyed, 101
outlive, 100
out of it, 36
outreach, 100
  mission denominational, 103
overpowering, 133
overreacting, 89
  you are, 24
overworking, 45
Owning, 38
Oxford, 126, 133

P
pace
  fast, 17
  slow, 109
pain, 15, 27–28, 50–52, 57, 77, 79, 83, 89–90, 120, 123–25, 129, 136
  inner, 15
  physical, 45
  thinking, 52
pairs, 56, 95
pale skin, 44
panic attacks, 44
Papeo, 147
paraphrase Jim, 10
parents, 57, 61–63, 122
  anxious, 37
  older, 96
  overbooked, 62

parents set, 62
parishioners, 38, 49, 92
park, 93
  camping, 42
Parson's Porch Books, 2
participation, 70
partner, 24
  abusive, 49
passionate joy, 127
passions, 13, 15
  creative, 127
  misdirected, 69
passive aggressiveness, 100
pass scrutiny, 45
past experience, 52
past hurts, 52, 57
pastoral ministers, effective, 34
pastoral visionary, 126
pastor functions, 74
pastor jobs, 42
pastor questions, 16
to pastor real people, unfit, 33
pastors, 30–33, 36–38, 42, 44–45, 47–49, 65, 67, 71–72, 74–78, 87, 92, 97–98, 103, 116, 118
  anxious, 103
  gathered, 72
  kind, 93
  male, 121
  retired, 113
  young, 101
Pastors and church members, 92

pastors experience, 75
pastor's family, 25
pastors feeling, 37
pastors judge, 116
Pastors of fear, 41
Pastors of strong
integrity, 118
past regrets, 123
pasture, 75
  put out to, 113
path, 41, 43
Pathological stuff, 64
pathology, 35, 64
patience, 36, 69, 71
Patterns of Church
Polity, 146
Paul, 46, 60, 68, 71, 77,
81, 94, 113, 115, 120,
122, 147
Paulist Press, 146
peace, 59, 62–63, 69, 71,
77, 93, 96, 123, 128, 138
peach ice cream, 127
Peale, 29
Penitentes, 124
People, 31, 34, 36, 49,
53, 55–56, 58–59, 74, 89,
91, 117, 122, 129, 132–
33
perceptions, 88, 91, 103–
4
permission, 2, 34
permit Satan, 79
perpetrating, 28
perpetual fighting
modes, 31
perplexities, 79

persecutions, 77
persevere, 72, 100
person, 20, 22, 25, 31,
36, 59, 69, 83, 87, 116,
122–23, 129, 131, 135,
137
  bad, 109
  first, 73, 149
  guilty, 121
  hurting, 96
  proud, 76
  right, 52
  wrong, 76
  young, 33
personal circle, 30
personal effectiveness,
37
personal guilt, 110
personality, 19
perspectives, 15, 32, 38,
41, 46, 116
pews, 93, 129
Phillips Brooks, 48, 91
phobia, 44
photocopying, 2
physical appearance, 57
physical characteristics,
52
physical issues, 16
physicians, 45, 85, 149
pied piper, 98
Pilgrim Presbyterian
Church, served, 36
Pilgrim Press, 145–46
pitch, 29
pitchers, 29
  modern, 29

pitching, 29
planting seeds, 73
Po, 145
pointless rebellion, 63
poles, opposite, 60
political fake news, 31
politics, 30, 75
Polo, 5
positivity, 11, 126
Post-Traumatic Church Syndrome, 147
pouring gasoline, 31
power, 19, 45, 62, 65, 67, 71, 75–76, 78, 112
power groups use guilt, 142
power issues, 37
powerlessness, 64, 76
powers and principalities, 65
Practical Christianity, 29
Practical Christianity in New York, 149
practice praying, 96
practice self-flagellation, 124
praise, 78, 80–81
pray, 45, 78–79, 81, 106–8
prayer meetings, 78, 101
prayers, 11, 70, 78, 80–81, 106, 138
  anxious, 70
preach, 30, 32–33, 36, 59, 98, 118, 129
preacher, 48–49, 70, 92, 126, 132, 149
  educated, 34
  right, 124
preach forgiveness, 121
preaching, 48, 58, 91–92, 99, 113, 138, 144, 146
precious possession, 129
precondition, 47
predecessor, 67
predictions, 89
premature aging, 42
preoccupation, 119
Presbyterian pastor, 58
prescription drugs, 120
pressure, 85
  high blood, 44
Preventing Sexual Abuse in Congregations, 146
price, 50, 62, 133
pride, 23, 29, 59–60, 122
  label, 60
  unhealthy, 122
pride goeth before a fall, 23, 60
prince, 70, 75
prison, 70, 74, 77, 123
private feeling, 67
problems, 18, 27, 29, 37, 51, 75, 79, 90, 94, 118, 122, 136
  drug, 120
  money, 88
  real, 37, 87
  reason, 90
  root, 97
  trust, 76
process, 22, 52, 98
  active, 50

emotional, 96
slow, 109
productive time, 99
productive ways, 44
professed Christian, 134
professing member, 75
professional help, 88
professionals, 33, 87
  underequipped, 32
project, 56, 85
promiscuity, 22
promises, 80, 86, 95, 100, 107
  professional, 92
prosperous state, 25
prostitution, 132
protection plan, 124
protective shield, 91
Proverbs, 23, 60
  taped, 38
Providence, 48
psalmist words, 80
psalms, 78–80
  happy, 79
  negative, 79
psalms focus, 80
Psalter, 79
Psy, 148
psychiatrist, 44
psychological issues, 51
Psychologists, 68
psychology, 94
  shared, 126
Psychology and healthy ministers, 114
psychopaths, 108
psychotherapist, 42, 99

psychotic cases, 62
punishment, 123–24
  anticipated, 124
  punish ourselves, 124
pursued joy, first, 149
Putting the hurt on people, 53
puzzle learning, painful, 89

Q
Quantico, 109
quit, 95, 113

R
race, 57–58, 136
Rachael, 146
radiant bliss, 128
rage, 14, 22, 53–55, 60, 63–64
Rainer Maria, 147
Ramsey, Nancy, 146
Random House, 145
Reba, 147
rebellion, full-scale, 112
recycle guilt, 108
redefinition, 87
redemption, 27, 124
referrals, 77, 92
reformer Martin Luther, 108
refuge, 26, 135
Region, 65
regrets, 11, 15, 50
rejection, 17, 57, 76, 89, 97
rejection lights, 45

rejoice, 27, 59
rejuvenating, 59
relationships, 17, 31, 35, 37, 51–53, 70, 96, 118, 121
　broken, 96
　human, 21
　intimate, 35
　marital, 117
　normal, 118
　restorative, 135
　restoring, 96
　right, 48
　sever, 92
relax, 46, 51
reliance, 56, 79
religion, 43, 58, 62, 68
　organized, 43
religion class, 94
religious sects, 43, 124
religious sects teach, 124
Religious Systems, 145
relive, 46
remind, 81, 126
re-parenting, 21
representatives, 104
repressed feelings, 65
repressing, 56, 58
Repression, 15
resent hearing, 124
resistance, 73, 98
resource, 20, 127
responsibility, 33, 76–77, 119–20
restitution, 123
restoration, 26, 90
resurrection, bodily, 107

retirement time, 64
retreats, 122
　weekend, 106
retribution, 52
retrieval system, 2
revivals, 110, 132
reward, 128, 134
Ridgecrest Baptist Church, 5
righteous, 26, 69
Riley, 147
Rilke, 147
Rio Grande, 132
risk, 66, 146
　emotional, 91
ritual site, 124
Rivers Baptist Church, 5
road sign pointing, 137
Robert, 146
Robert Louis Stevenson, 137
rocks, 41, 124
Romans, 122
　immortal, 81
Ron, 146
room, 68, 89
root, 61, 89
rulers lord, 66
Rumors, 75
Russia, 21
Russian Theological Academy, 21

S

sacred values elicit, 130
sadness, 87, 138
Safe Sanctuaries, 146

Safety, 88
Saint Francis, 138
Saint Joseph, 5
Saint Joseph State Hospital, 36
Saint Paul, 33
Saint Petersburg, 21
saints, 26
salvation, 115, 137
Sanctification, 108
sanctification masquerade, 109
sang, 36, 93
Savannah, 5
scars, 50, 76–77
school form, elementary, 118
School of Practical Christianity in New York, 149
Schools, 29
scriptures, 32, 39, 47, 68, 82, 107, 137
scriptures call, 89
Scrooge, 19
   miser Ebenezer, 19
searches, 32, 85, 120
sea shore, 134
Seasoned ministers, 73
seasons, dry, 72
secret jealousy, 45
secret pond, 102
secrets, 19, 86, 114, 120, 124, 145
seductive intensities, 112
seekers hop, 32
self, 37, 61

real, 61
self-abandonment, 55
self-awareness, 65
self-control, 56
   exercise, 116
self-defeating, 63
self-determination, 74
   limitless, 64
self-esteem, 37, 109
self-image, inadequate, 74
self-interests, 31
selfish feelings, 72
self-mutilation, 22
self-preservation, 47
self-reinforcing, 18
self-respect, 110–11
self-righteous, 22, 115
seminaries, 33–34, 45, 75, 79, 134
seminary graduates, 75
   evaluated, 33
seminary training, 33
sensations, 119, 128
sensitivity, 119
sensuality, 24, 60, 126
separateness, 56
separation, 70, 122, 124
separation insurance, 124
sermons, 36, 68, 114, 121, 126–27
   first, 86, 99
   guilt-producing, 110
Servant Leadership, 146
servants, 66, 132, 149
service, 15, 17, 26, 75, 99, 127

sex, 24, 35, 116–17
  avoiding, 116
sex preoccupation, 118
sex trafficking, 120
Sexual Abuse and Healing, 146
sexual awareness, 116
sexual cues signaling, 118
sexual difficulties, 117
sexual identity, healthy, 119
sexual immorality, 120
sexual innuendo, 120
sexual interest, 119
sexual issues, 119
sexuality, 24, 115–20, 122
  exercise, 119
  healthy, 116
sexuality arouses suspicion, 118
sexual misconduct, 67
sexual safety, 122
Sexual temptation, 119
Sexual Violence, 145
sex wanting, opposite, 120
shadows, 122
  dark, 129
shame, 66, 68, 101, 110–17, 119–23, 125
  applying, 112
  authentic, 111–12
  inauthentic, 112
  internalized, 112
  use, 111
  welcome, 111, 113

Shame-based fear, 112
shame reminds, 111
share Christ, 133
Shared Grace, 145
share joy, 9
sheep stealing, 31
sheer numbers, 85
Shine, 146
showcase dysfunction, 19
sickness, 65, 72
  suffering, 113
signal, 40, 99
silence, 24, 32, 35, 85, 113, 115, 127
Simon & Schuster, 147
sinful nature, 120, 122
sinful tendencies, 109
sinners, 26, 69, 124
Sin Revisited, 145
sins, 24, 61, 68, 72, 79, 108–9, 114–15, 117, 123–24
  deadly, 23–24, 59–61, 69
  eternal, 115
  sexual, 119
  unpardonable, 114–15
sisters, 26, 113
situations, 11, 18, 37, 40, 51–52, 67, 78, 84, 86, 92, 115, 120, 130
  anger-generating, 55
  bad, 38
  crappy, 72
  hard, 38
  living, 51

novel, 41
size
  limited, 37
  middle, 33
sized stature, 49
skills, 13, 66, 112
sloth, 25, 59–61
slum area, 134
smelling roses, 127
snow, 97
snowy conditions, 97
social anxiety, 84, 89, 106
social anxiety disorder, 84
social feeling, 71
social situations, 14, 84
social worlds, 14
society, 31–32, 64, 114
  extroverted, 84
Softcover, 2
son, 21, 94, 102
songs, 30
  person singing
worship, 26
sorrows, 66, 70, 79
souls, 14, 18, 22, 38, 51, 68, 88, 108, 110–11
  inner, 53
  prodigal, 25
soul-searching, 115
soul's perimeter, 55
sound, 79, 119
  crucified, 66
source, 50, 52, 75, 118, 120
  best, 77

South Carolina, 127
Southern Baptist Convention, 124
Southern Baptist Theological Seminary, 71
Southminster Presbyterian Church, 5
space, 38, 136
  personal, 90
Spheres, 136
spiritual abusers, 115
Spiritual abusers tap, 110
spiritual atmosphere, safe, 135
spiritual bankruptcy, 122
spiritual director redirect, 77
spiritual disability, 70
spiritual gatherings, 70
spiritual life, 114
spiritual longings, 110
spiritual mystery, 66
spiritual poison, 28
spiritual question, 70
spiritual ritual, 32
spiritual snare, 123
Spiritual Struggle, 115
spontaneity, 23
spots and wrinkles, 39
spouse, 62
  avaricious, 25
  slothful, 25
Spurgeon, Charles, 32, 48, 70, 86
squishy feelings, 108
staff turnover, high, 19
started worship, 80

start ministry, 34
state championship, 98
state hospital, 36
status quo, 41
stay out of the fool, 38
stealthily commandeer, 19
stepping, 104
stepping down, 104
stewardship, 103
stomach, 44, 106, 133
stone, first, 61
Stoner, Chad, 72
Stony Brook Church in Omaha, 72
stop hurting, 46
stories, 18, 61, 79, 102, 131, 133
  fake, 47
  horrible, 64
stories pull, 129
strangers, 104, 131
strategies, ineffective, 50
strength, 17, 56, 59, 64, 70, 73, 75, 77, 79, 81, 85, 96, 100, 113, 117
  primary, 34
  ultimate, 122
stress, 47, 51, 62, 75, 83, 85–86
  best, 86
  financial, 51
  intense, 74
strong integrity, 118
studied Rembrandt's painting, 21
stuff, 105

stuff perpetuates anxiety, 105
subject, 10–11, 34, 39
  hard, 34
  uncomfortable, 116
suburban church, large, 33
Suicide, 42
Sunday, 27, 36, 93, 98–99, 101, 121, 149
Sunday brunch, 30
Sunday mornings, 30, 40, 59
Sunday worship, 42
suns, 68, 136
supernatural, 95
supply-demand mitigates, 103
supportive faith group, 27
Suppress, 72
Suppressing anger, 53
suppression, 94
surge, energetic, 18
surprise, 11, 36, 69, 126
Surprised, 133
surprise factor, 37
surroundings, 73
symptoms, 44, 55, 60, 68, 85
  common, 44

T
talented minister, 67
tangles, 18
  emotional, 18
tap, 46, 126

taste, unique, 120
Tasting, 127
tea, 99
teacher, 111, 124, 149
teaching church groups, 55
televisions, 25, 61, 94
temper, 54–55, 63
Templeton Foundation, 13
temporary feelings, 28
temptations, 23, 108–9, 111, 116–17
Tennessee, 5, 25, 145, 149
Tennessee Citadel Park Baptist Chapel, 5
Tennessee First Baptist Church, 5
Tennessee Lakewood Baptist Church, 5
Tennessee Medical School, 46
Tennessee Rich Valley United Methodist Church, 5
tension, 57, 87, 90–91, 98, 101
territories, 19, 144
testimony, 37, 99
Texas, 132
Texas churches, 132
Tex Sample, 33
thanksgiving, 40, 78, 80
Thea, 146
them asking, 103

theologian Paul Tillich, 96
Theologian Rob Bell, 130
Theologian Soren Kierkegaard, 95
therapeutic treatment, 97
therapist, 13, 36, 44, 46, 61, 88–89, 113–14, 124, 145, 149
  psychiatric, 15, 62, 88
therapy, 44, 88–90
  cognitive, 46
  exposure, 44
  prescribed physical, 85
therapy work, 43
this son of yours, 22
threats, 42, 96
  direct, 51
Thy will be done, 81
Tillich, 147
time bomb, 58
time machine, universal, 135
tone, 16, 52, 85
tools, 40, 58, 101, 113
torture chamber, 91
town, 43, 45, 99, 130
Toxic church groups and religious sects teach, 124
Toxic congregations, 30–31
Toxicity, 7, 13, 31
Toxic shame, 122
traditions, 28, 74, 100–101
tragic wound, 77

training ground, 26
transition, 104, 121
transparency, 65
traps, 19, 119
trauma, 20
  church-based, 44
  sexual, 119
traumatizing event, 44
treasures, 105
  empty, 105
treasures clogging, worldly, 105
tree limb, 102
trees, 102
trials, 78, 113
tribulation, 70
Trinity Church, 48
trust, 26, 46, 67, 107
Trusting God, 97
truth, 32, 37, 50, 72, 86, 88–89, 117, 146
  new, 103
Truth and Light Church, 133
Tuesday, 149
tune piano, 36
twelve-million-dollar study, 13
Tyler, 99
tyrants, 23, 60, 66

U
ultimate, 61, 128
ultimate destruction, 117
unavoidable topic, 116
unchangeable features, 57
Uncontrolled anger, 61, 69
Uncovering, 44
Understanding Clergy Misconduct, 145
unfaithfulness, 80
unhappiness, 28
  utter, 15
Unhealthy churches reject, 135
United Church Press, 146
United Methodist, 33
United Methodist Church, 103
  progressive, 68
United States, 34, 96, 107, 134
  affluent, 133
University, 46, 71, 126, 133
University of Tennessee, 149
University Press, 147
unorganized crowd, 84
unrighteousness, 123
unsolicited names, 103
use food, 60
use force, 90

V
values, 32, 125, 130
  positive, 130
  professes, 130
  sacred, 130
Vanderbilt, 29

Vanderbilt Divinity School, 104
Vanderbilt University Divinity School, 149
Varieties, 146
Verdad, 133
victims, 19, 24, 35, 61, 146
   silenced, 25
videos, 52, 77
   fearful, 46
Vintage Books, 147
violence, 60, 111
   domestic, 53, 146
violent terms, 24
Virginia, 5, 34, 101, 146
Virginia First Baptist Church, 5
Virginia Washington Chapel United Methodist Church, 5
vision, 17, 37, 70, 91, 112, 126, 130
   effective, 17
   minister's, 111
Visionquests, 24
   weekend, 25
vivid visitations, 19
voice, 16, 52, 125
   raising, 69
vulnerability, 9, 65–66, 76, 91, 118, 136, 144
   emotional, 47
vulnerable times, 78

W
Waiters, 24
Wallowing, 123
walls, 53, 65, 76, 91
   negative emotional, 29
Warich Chapel, 36
Warich Chapel services, 36
warmth, 51, 126
wave, new, 65
weaknesses, 77–78
Weeping Water, 36, 78
weight, 26, 72
welcome, 90, 104, 135
welcomed Paul, 113
welcoming adjustment, 101
Wesley, 113
Westminster Baptist Chapel, 5
Westminster Confession, 39, 134
Westside Church, 93
what if scenarios, 94
when i prayed, 10
wholeheartedness, 130
wholeness, 116
   restoring, 113
Williamson, 147
Willpower, 82
Wilmington, 45
Win-Win World, 146
wisdom, 32, 56, 64, 100, 125, 130
withdrawals, 51, 63
wives, 47
Wolfe, Kenneth, 137

woman, 26, 35–36, 46, 53, 58, 71, 94, 121, 123, 132
  anxious, 93
  single, 26
  weak, 89
  young, 116
women, 24, 35, 59, 63–65
  angry, 64
  young, 134
women abusers, 35
women's clothing, 76
Woodlawn Baptist Church, 5
words, gentle, 38
words stir, hard, 38
work, 25, 27, 50, 62, 74–75, 98–99, 109, 128–29, 131
  excellent, 127
work hazard, 72
work-related issues, 51
world, 10–11, 19, 23, 25, 27, 31, 56–58, 60–61, 70, 75, 110–11, 115, 133, 138, 144
  inner, 16
  real, 128
World Council, 146
world countries, 132
world hungering, 17
world peace, 71
world religions, 43
World War II, 101
world wars, 127
worriers, extreme, 89
Worries, 105
worry, 79, 85, 88–89, 95, 97, 106
worship, 28, 30, 32, 36, 59, 93–94, 98, 133
wrath, 24, 38, 41, 58, 63
wrestling, 62, 98
writer publishing, 126
writers, 24, 113, 149
  first Christian, 133
wrong word, single, 38
www.parsonsporchbooks.com, 2
Wytheville, 5

Y
Yale, 147
ye kind, 58
yes to the Mess, 72
Young Poet, 147
youth, 15, 30, 35, 62–63, 98, 101, 118
  attracted, 98
youth crusades, 132
youth director, 99
youth group, 30
youth work, 37

Z
Zarra, 147
Zephaniah, 137
Zion United Chur
Zondervan, 145
zone, safe, 47

www.ingramcontent.com/pod-product-compliance
Lightning Source LLC
Chambersburg PA
CBHW052132110526
44591CB00012B/1687